I'M NO HERO

19-34

ETHEL BARRETT

A Regal Venture Book
A Division of G/L Publications
Glendale, California, U.S.A.

Second Printing, 1974
Third Printing, 1975

Published by Regal Books Division, G/L Publications
Glendale, California 91209
Printed in U.S.A.

Library of Congress Catalog Card No. 73-85395
ISBN 0-8307-0254-7

The Scripture versions used in *I'm No Hero!* include:
  King James Version
  The Living Bible, Paraphrased (Wheaton:
  Tyndale House, Publishers, 1971). Used
  by permission.
  The Amplified Bible (Grand Rapids: Zondervan
  Publishing House, 1965). Used by permission.

Contents

This book may be used by teachers and students as a resource for the G/L Bible study *Men of Courage* (Course 52). Available from your church supplier.

Who Wants to Be a Hero?

"Well, I do, actually. I say outwardly, in front of my friends, that I don't, but inside I really would like to be brave and strong and dauntless—you know, one of these people who never make a mistake, or hardly ever. But inside I sometimes just feel like a blob. When I read about great men and women in history, and especially in the Bible, they seem sort of unreal, as if somebody painted a beautiful picture but no person could ever really be like that. And if they are real, then who could measure up? These men and women in the Bible seem so perfect. They never make a mistake, they never do anything wrong, they're never frightened. They're *dauntless**—that's the word for it, I guess. If dauntless is the word, then count me out; I sure have plenty of "daunt." If it took great heroes like that to get God's work done, how could He possibly ever use a person like me?"

The answer is of course that God always has used people just like you. They were heroes all right, because He made

*Without fear.

them heroes, but they were far from perfect. One of the most wonderful things about being a Christian is that God has always used ordinary men and women and ordinary boys and girls to get His work done. They had their fears and their weaknesses and their misgivings and, yes, they had their failures too. They had in fact the same hang-ups as you may have. Whatever is "bugging" you was "bugging" them. For the truth is that there is no other way for God to get His work done except through imperfect human beings. Indeed He has chosen this way to do it. So when you get discouraged or feel inadequate, or when you get discouraged with *other* Christians, think of this:

God is still recruiting from the human race.

Remember this.

Then you won't get too critical of others.

And you won't get too discouraged with yourself.

Introduction

This is a book of astonishing adventure. It's a book of flooding rivers to cross, of crashing walls, of battles and spies, and a donkey that talked, and strange dreams—

But mostly it's a story of people who became heroes— people who were the most unlikely candidates for heroes that you could imagine.

There was a man who felt he could never become a hero because he was the least important one in his family. And a woman who became a heroine* simply because there was no one else around to do the job. And a man who had to be constantly prodded by God: "Don't be afraid, I'll be with you. Be strong, now, I'm right here. Buck up and get on with it."

And there were many more.

As you read about them, you might recognize yourself— your own fears and your own misgivings and your own shortcomings. For though each of these people did marvelous things, they were, after all, only "people"—just like you.

*A lady hero

They were great merely because they allowed God to work through them.

Take a good look at these people and learn something from them.

For God is still looking for heroes.

And who knows?

The next great hero may be you!

1

Temper Is Spelled T-R-O-U-B-L-E

Numbers 20

"But I Have This Temper, You See"

"Actually I think I'm hyper-active. My grandmother says I'm 'high-strung'—you know, a thoroughbred. My dad is a little more blunt about it. He says I have a short fuse which means it doesn't take much to make me explode. My Aunt Joan says I'm always putting my foot in my mouth, which means I'm always saying the wrong thing. All I know is I'm always saying things I wish I hadn't said. And I think, 'Why did I have to go and say that.' But then it's too late."

Yes. That's the problem. After you've lost your temper, it usually *is* too late. Of course, a short temper is a nuisance and a bore and there is no reason why you should have to put up with the culprit in the first place. You're too nice a person and too smart to be bothered with such nonsense. Carrying a temper around is like trying to swim upstream with a stone tied around your neck, you just can't make any headway.

But more about that later.

Temper Is Spelled T-r-o-u-b-l-e

Of course, temper is a state of mind; you can have a sweet and even temper just as easily as a bad one,* but usually when we say, "He has a temper," or, "He lost his temper," we're talking about anger and it means nothing but trouble. And if you have one, you are not alone. It happens to the best people, sometimes even the greatest leaders.

There was a man once who lost his temper and he did it right out in front of everybody and it created quite a dramatic splash. And he was one of the greatest leaders the world has ever known.

His name was Moses.

"Not Moses!?!"

Well, it does give you a bit of a jolt, for he was known as the gentlest, kindest man on earth. The Bible tells us he was meek, and it's best to get it straight right off that "meek" does NOT mean "weak." It means gentle, kind and *humble*. And you can be as strong as an ox, as swift as an eagle, and have a brain like a computer and still be gentle, kind and humble.

You just wouldn't expect anybody like that to lose his temper, ever. But Moses did. And this is how it happened.

This Is What Led Up to It

It happened very nearly at the end of Moses' story. It's a long story, too long to tell here except for a brief rundown.

The Israelites were God's chosen people. And when they were slaves in Egypt under a wicked Pharaoh, God chose Moses to lead them out of slavery and into a land He had promised to give them. When Pharaoh chased them, God

*Well, almost as easily.

2

made a pathway through the Red Sea for them to get across, and then closed the waters so Pharaoh's soldiers could not follow them. He guided them with a pillar of cloud by day and a pillar of fire by night. When they were thirsty He sent them water. When they were hungry He sent them manna from heaven. He provided for them every step of the way.

And every step of the way they grumbled.

You'd think that when they got to the Promised Land they would shape up and smile.

Not so.

They sent twelve spies in to look over the land. And though the spies came back with fruit so marvelous that one cluster of grapes had to be carried on a pole between two men, their report was ominous.*

"The people are like giants," they gloomed.

"The cities are surrounded by thick walls," they glummed.

"We felt like grasshoppers before them! They would crush us!" they bellowed.**

And the grumbling spread through the whole camp of Israelites like one big wail. There was the Promised Land they'd been waiting for but they didn't want to go over because they were afraid. And there was God waiting to help them, but they didn't let Him because they didn't believe.

So God gave them what they wanted. He let them go back and wander in the wilderness again. For forty years.

And for forty years they grumbled.

Now forty years is a long time, so the adults got old and died, and their children grew up. And they roamed from place to place, looking for pasture for their animals. They had to keep moving. The story of their lives was "March—stop—march." Or, "Hurry up and wait." This they did, until

*That means, from doomsville.

**Two spies said, "Let's go! We can take it!" More about them later.

3

finally they found themselves at Kadesh. And where was Kadesh? Why, right back where they were before—right on the edge of the Promised Land!

And they were still grumbling.

This time they had no water.

"I Wish I Were Dead!"

Ever say this? It goes along with throwing yourself on the couch (or on the floor if nothing else is handy) and pounding your clenched fists on whatever's there. The object is to frighten your parents out of their wits. And the reason for doing it usually boils down to one thing: everything isn't going your way. If you ever catch yourself doing this, stop and think. Hasn't God worked things out for you before?* Well, then, won't He do it again? Isn't He still running things right on schedule?

You wouldn't think so, the way some of us act.

The Israelites were no different. God had given them water before.** He had worked out all their problems and supplied all their needs. But, did they remember this and trust Him to do it again?

No. They held a protest meeting.

"Why did you make us leave Egypt?"

"You've brought us here to get rid of us!"

"Where is the fertile land you told us about?"

"Why, there isn't even enough water to drink!"

They complained. They accused. They mocked. And yes, they even wailed, "We wish we were dead!!!"

Moses sighed. He was weary. Weary of these people. And weary of their complaining.

---

*Of course you have to **give Him** the problem first; that only makes sense.

**See Exodus 17

4

If You Can Keep Your Head—

Like the poem* says: "If you can keep your head, when all about you are losing theirs and blaming it on you—"

Moses kept his head. He went to the Tabernacle with his brother Aaron, and there they knelt and asked God what to do. "Take the rod**," the Lord told them. "Then call all the people together. As they watch, speak to that rock over there and tell it to pour out water!"

So Moses began to obey. "Take the rod," God had said. He took the rod from the place where it was kept in the Tabernacle. "Call the people." He had the trumpets blown and called the great congregation together. They came from every direction, all of them, every grumbling, complaining, long-faced one of them.

And then it happened.

"Speak to the rock," God had said.

"Something in Me Just Snapped!"

"I don't know how it ever happened. I didn't mean to lose my temper. It was as if the pressure had built up so I felt like a steam boiler. Something had to give!"

Yes, it does happen. The pressure builds up just so long and then you pop a cork somewhere and you can hardly believe the person who is screaming is you.

Moses stood up there by that rock and looked down at the people, at their scowling faces and their droopy wind-blown sand-blasted beards. There were so many of them they looked like a vast sea of faces. And all their rudeness and all their disbelief and all their stubbornness just hit him like a tidal wave.

*"If"—Rudyard Kipling
**This is the rod Moses had from the beginning, the one he used to touch the Red Sea.

"Listen, you REBELS!" he shouted, "Must we bring you water from this rock?!?"

Then he lifted the rod and—

WHAM!

Struck the rock with all his might. And—

WHAM!

Again he struck it.

Moses, the strongest leader, and the meekest man in all the earth, had lost his temper.

"God Still Kept His Promise?"

And then—out of that rock—swirling, bubbling, foaming, tumbling—came—

WATER!

The people cupped their hands and drank it and splashed it over their faces. They shouted in astonishment and ran in confusion to fetch jugs and vessels to fill with it. They backed off, pushing each other to make way for it. And it kept coming and coming from that rock, a vast amount of water, enough for all the people and their cattle.

But Moses had lost his temper.

"What's the Harm?"

"What's the harm in what Moses did? The people got their water and things were better than they'd been before. What's all the fuss about his temper? After all he put up with, it's about time he blew up. It's a wonder he didn't do it sooner."

Well, actually it *is* a wonder he didn't do it sooner. From where we're looking at it, he had every right to be angry. But there are some loose threads here that ought to be tied up before we draw a conclusion. There's more here than meets the eye.

Moses put himself on equal footing with God. "Must *we*

fetch water?" he shouted. *We?* Who was going to perform this miracle anyhow? And who did Moses think he was?

And Moses struck the rock, not once, but twice, instead of just speaking to it as God had told him to do. There doesn't seem to be any harm in that, until you stop to think about it.

In the midst of all that confusion and complaining and unbelief, God wanted the leader to be cool, calm and collected. He wanted Moses to stand quietly by that rock and speak to it calmly. And there, before that multitude of skeptics*, the water would pour forth, and God would be glorified, and His kindness would be made known and there would be no doubt in the people's minds that He still cared and He was still running things.

So you can see that when Moses shouted "We!" and whammed that rock, he really blew it.

God kept His promise all right. He was faithful. The Bible tells us, ". . . and the water gushed out; and the people and their cattle drank. BUT—"

Ah, here it is. The payoff, as they say today. The consequences.

"But . . . because you did not believe Me and did not honor Me before the Israelites . . . you shall not lead these people into the Promised Land."

The Israelites were going to get into the Promised Land, all right. But Moses and Aaron would not be with them.

"Isn't That Punishment a Bit Stiff?"

Well it would seem like it. But stop and think. When God chooses leaders He gives a great deal *to* them. So He expects a great deal *from* them. And one of the things He expects is absolute obedience.

Shortly after this, Aaron died, and the people mourned him tor thirty days. And Moses knew that before long God

*People who say, "I don't believe it; show me!"

would call him home too. He was not to go into the Promised Land. God loved him just as much. And he was still a great leader. But disobedience had to be punished.

"But Can't a Person Get Angry?"

Of course. And we all do, at times. Anyone who says he *never* gets angry about *anything* is a phony. But the Bible tells us, "When you get angry, do not sin; do not ever let your anger . . . last until the sun goes down."*

"When I get angry, I can't sin? But that's when I *want* to shout, to be sassy, to disobey, to stamp my foot, to—"

Of course. Because when you're angry you're not thinking too clearly. You can make every mistake in the book. And there's a reason.

When your mind tells your body it is angry, your body gets busy. Your tiny adrenal glands pour out adrenalin into your bloodstream, and everything goes into first gear, like racing your motor. Your heart beats faster, your blood pumps hard and fast through your veins, your stomach ties in a square knot and you breathe harder. Everything in you wants to *do* something about it. When you say you feel like a boiler building up pressure, you are not far wrong. Your body is filled with excess energy** and if you don't do *something* you'll explode!

The idea is to do something worthwhile! Like the three-spined stickleback.*** What? You never heard of a three-spined stickleback? Well, it's a fish with a hot temper, very scrappy indeed. And the three-spined stickleback digs its nest in the sandy bottom of shallow water. And if another three-spined stickleback digs its nest too close, the two of

*Ephesians 4:26 **(Amplified)**
**Get-up-and-GO!
***Try reading this fast.

8

them chase each other back and forth from nest to nest. But neither one hurts the other. They finish off the chase by glaring at each other halfway between the nests, bubbling and frothing. And then they do a nose dive, stand on their heads—and start frantically digging holes in the sand! So they've got rid of all that excess "steam" and no harm is done.

Of course you are going to get angry some times. And if you do, naturally you can't dig holes in the sand under water with your nose. So go punch your punching bag. Or run up and down the beach, or up and down a hill. Or bat your tennis ball up against the house. Or shovel some snow. Or clean up your room, get your desk organized. Or jump rope.*

There's a Better Way

Of course, the closer you are to God, the fewer times you'll be angry. But if you do get angry, ask Him to help you when you feel the first warning signs. Then your mind won't get a chance to tell your body to get going and the adrenalin won't make your heart beat fast and your stomach tie up in a square knot. Save you a lot of trouble.

Away with It!

So away with temper! It's doing you no good. Like we said in the beginning, a short temper is a nuisance and a bore and there is no reason why you should have to put up with it. You're too nice a person and too smart to be bothered with such nonsense. Carrying a temper around is like trying to swim upstream with a stone tied around your neck; you just can't make any headway.

Just give it to God. And then you *can't* lose it.

*Stay away from dishes; your mother might have good china.

9

2
Maybe I Can
Patch This Up Myself

Numbers 21:1-9; John 3:13-18

The Israelites were out early as usual that morning, gathering manna. And as usual, they were grumbling. Now once you begin to grumble, the list can become longer and longer until there's no end to it. And theirs did.

The king of Edom wouldn't let them go through his land.

The king of Edom wouldn't let them go through his land and they had to take a long tiresome detour.

The king of Edom wouldn't let them go through his land and they had to take a long tiresome detour, and there were high winds and wild sandstorms.

The king of Edom wouldn't let them go through his land and they had to take a long tiresome detour and sometimes there were high winds and wild sandstorms and the pesky Canaanites had attacked them and the way was hot and dry and lonely and there wasn't a tree in sight and never

11

enough water and Moses and all their leaders were bullies and nobody was getting along with anybody and the whole camp was going to the dogs and that manna—Yaaaaak—that manna—they were getting sick of it and—

Well, you can see how it is. Once you get the hang of griping, you can keep so busy at it that there is practically no time for you to do anything else.

So, of course, you can't get any joy out of life.

And there's no time to *thank* God for all the *good* things He has done for you.

Now it's pretty hard to weary God. He has no end of patience with our mistakes and shortcomings, and yes, even our disobedience.* But if there is one thing that *can* weary Him, it would be grumbling.

Anyhow their list of gripes had become longer with every passing day. And they were up with the dawn that morning to gather manna and to get an early start on their grumbling. Where *was* God, anyhow? Was He even listening? And when was He going to start answering their requests and straightening things out?

He was listening. And the answer was sudden.

Tsssssssst!!!

One of them stopped short, a sharp stinging pain in his ankle. Hot, like fire.

Before it slithered away, he saw it.

It was a snake.

He howled with pain.

"What was it?" a fellow gathering manna nearby called out. "Are you hurt?"

"It's a snake! I've been bitten!"

Then there was another howl of pain nearby. And another. Then howls from everywhere.

Snakes! The whole area was infested with them!

*If it's temporary. Don't push Him too far.

Maybe It Will Go Away

Those who had been bitten limped painfully back to their tents. And the news dribbled in from every section of the camp. People everywhere, all over the entire camp were being bitten. The wails could be heard for miles. And the grumbling too. Now they had one *more* thing to add to their list. All their other hardships—and now this!

Oh, well. Maybe by tomorrow it would go away.

But it didn't go away.

Maybe We Can Patch It Up Ourselves

The people who hadn't been bitten bathed the wounds, and did whatever they knew how to do for snakebites.

By afternoon, the camp was nearly silent. The people who had been bitten were at the doors of their tents, to catch whatever breeze there might be. And they were desperately sick with raging fevers. By nightfall, the wails of sorrow rose in the desert air.

The people who had been bitten, were dead.

They couldn't "patch it up" themselves.

It Isn't Going to Go Away!

There was little sleep in the camp that night. The snakes were everywhere—they had to be beaten off. The next few days were like a nightmare.

And then the truth dawned on them.

Disobedience and grumbling had always got them into trouble. And now they'd done it again.

Always before, God had let their enemies overrun them. This time He had allowed their *natural* enemies to overrun them.

Snakes.

And they weren't going to go away.

13

The snakes were a fact. How to get rid of them? What was the answer?

Is There a Remedy?

The people went to Moses. There was only one answer, and now they knew it. "We have sinned!" they cried, "We've complained against God and against you! Pray to Him and ask Him to take away the snakes!"

Moses did pray to God. And God answered, and gave him the remedy. And it was so simple, that it was hard to believe.

What's this? Take some bronze and make a bronze snake, just like the "fiery snakes" that were doing the biting?

Yes.

And attach it to the top of a pole?

Yes.

And anyone who has been bitten shall live if he *looks at* it?

Yes, yes, all of this.

And what's more, Moses did it.

It *didn't* seem to make sense. It wasn't an antidote for snakebite. But anyhow, Moses took God at His word, and did it. He took some bronze and made the snake. And attached it to a pole. And he lifted the pole up in a part of the camp where everyone could see it. For God had told him that everyone who would look at that snake would be cured. And He didn't mean a passing glance. He meant to *look* at it, knowing it was God's own remedy.

And what's more—*it worked!*

The Bible does not tell us that everyone who had been bitten was healed. It tells us that everyone who had been bitten was healed *when he looked at the bronze snake.*

There *was* a remedy!

14

But What Does It Mean?

What a story! And whatever did it mean?

Well, it does seem odd, that in the midst of all their great battles and unforgettable adventures—that *this* should happen. And it takes up only five verses in the Bible. You could skip right over it and hardly know it was there at all.

But actually it is important. And it was not that easily forgotten. God had let all this happen for a very good reason.

The reason wasn't clear for hundreds of years!

And do you know Who made it clear?

Jesus Himself!

"Just as the bronze snake was the *only* remedy for the snakebite," He said, "I am the *only* remedy for sin. And just as that bronze snake had to be raised up on a pole for people to look at—I must be raised up on a cross, so that anyone who looks at Me *and believes in Me,* will have eternal life."*

Imagine!

God's remedy for the Israelites was a *picture* of what He intended to do hundreds of years later—a *picture* of Jesus on the cross, the only remedy for sin.

He was guilty of no sin. He bore *your* sins in His own body. . . . By *His* wounds, *you* are healed.** You have only to look to Him.

"But I'm No Sinner!"

The Bible says you are. "For all have sinned, and come short of the glory of God."*** If you're a part of the human race, that means you too.

Sorry about that.

*See John 3:14,15
**See 1 Peter 2:2-24.
***Romans 3:23

15

"Maybe I Can Patch It Up Myself"

Not so, not so. "Even if I said I was perfect—my own mouth would trip me up"*

You jolly well know it would. Or if your *mouth* didn't trip you up, your *thoughts* would.

Sorry about that too.

There's Only One Remedy

The Bible tells us: "There is salvation in no one else! Under all heaven there is no other name for men to call upon to save them."**

You see, this is quite a story after all! There's a great deal in it to remember.

And of all the things to remember, the most important one is—

God loves you.

Remember Jesus said that just as the snake had to be raised on a pole, *He* had to be raised on a cross? Well, right after that, and practically in the same breath, He added: "For God so loved the world that He gave His only begotten Son—that whosoever believeth on Him should not perish, but have everlasting life."!***

He will never *force* Himself on you, though. He will never bulldoze His way into your life.

Do you want Him for your Saviour?

The choice, of course, is yours.

*See Job 9:20.
**See Acts 4:12.
***John 3:16

3
I Want
to Serve God—*BUT*

Numbers 22:1-24; 23

"I Want to Serve God—But—"

"I want to serve God" is the part we talk about and sing
about, and sometimes even brag about. It's the "but" that
we keep to ourselves. Most of us would rather not let anyone know that there is a "but" in our lives. Sometimes we
don't even know the "but" is there, it keeps itself so well
hidden. Sometimes we know it's there all right—we just
don't like to admit it, even to ourselves. And it can be almost anything. "I want to serve God but—I still like to hang
around with these kids my parents don't approve of." "I
want to serve God but—I love clothes so much that I think
I go to church just to dress up and show off. But I wouldn't
want anybody to know it." Or, "I'd like to serve God but—if
it came to a showdown I'd really rather be popular. It's important to me right now to be popular." Or, "I'd like to serve
God but—if I don't do certain things and go along with the
gang, I won't be elected class president in my school."

Well, you get the idea. The "but" could be almost anything. Your "but" might not be the same as somebody
else's.*

*Everyone to his own "buts."

19

One thing, however, is for sure. In this chapter, "but" is a pesky little word that leads to nothing but trouble.

There was a man, once, who "wanted to serve God—but."

He was a prophet from Mesopotamia. The Israelites ran into him during their travels.

Or rather, *he* ran into *them*. In an indirect sort of way.

He was a fellow by the name of Balaam.

And this is how it happened.

The Israelites were fighting their way through enemy territory on their way to the Promised Land. They had defeated the Canaanites and the Amorites, and they were headed north in the direction of Moab.

And the king of Moab was terrified.

He was a fellow by the name of Balak.

The Israelites had conquered every country before them. Would they mow down Moab too?

Perhaps—perhaps—he could get some prophet to curse them.

Ahhh—*that* was it.

Send for a prophet to curse them. Send for Balaam!

And so we have the Israelites.

And a heathen king named Balak.

And a prophet named Balaam, who wanted to serve God—*but*.

These are our characters and this is our story.

Now when you tangle with a "but" in your life, it usually follows a pattern. This story follows a pattern, too. It begins with "I want to do it"—and goes on from there. Let's see how it works.

"I Want to Do It"

Now what it is you want to do, is not the question. The point is, it's not quite right, and down in your heart you know it. "But I want to do this thing. It may not be quite right—but there's nothing terribly *wrong* about it either.

20

And if I do it I'll be popular."*

That's exactly what crossed Balaam's mind when the messenger came from King Balak.

They explained to him about the Israelites, and how concerned King Balak was that they might just mow his kingdom down. Now Balak was very superstitious and he believed that if someone could *curse* the Israelites—

Well there seemed to be no *other* way to stop them.

Would Balaam curse them? This is what the messengers wanted to know.

Balaam thought about this for a moment, rocking back and forth, lost in deep thought. To curse the Israelites wasn't right, and he jolly well knew it. Still—Balak was a rich king, and the reward might be considerable—even great. The idea was attractive. *Very* attractive. He'd really like to do it.

"I'll See If It's Okay"

"This thing might be wrong" (you know it is). "But I'll ask the Lord about it. Yes, I'll really make it a matter of prayer."

Balaam went that route too. He entertained his important visitors, and while he was talking to them, his mind was going around like a whirligig. He knew the thing was wrong. But he hated to let *go* of the idea.

Now there's only one way to say "no." And that's to say it and mean it. If Balaam had only done this right off the bat, he would have saved himself a lot of trouble. But he didn't do it the easy way. He did it the long hard way. "Tarry here for the night," he told his visitors. "My servants will put you up. And I'll ask the Lord about it and let you know in the morning."

What?

*Or get rewards, or whatever.

21

Ask the Lord about it?!? Ask the Lord if he could curse the Lord's people?

How ridiculous!

But we're never more ridiculous than when we're trying to get away with something.

And Balaam was no exception.

He didn't know it yet, but he had started a long trek down hill.

"Don't Confuse Me with Facts"

The first thing we do when we are trying to get away with something, is gloss over the facts.* For if we get too involved with facts, we'll have to admit that what we want to do is wrong. The easiest way out is to just forget all the facts that make us uncomfortable.

That night, God said to Balaam, "Who are these men?"

Now God knew who these men were, and what they were up to. He just wanted Balaam to come out and admit it. But these were facts that Balaam didn't want to be confused with, so he started to gloss them over. "Oh," he said, "they've come from King Balak of Moab. The King says a vast horde of people from Egypt has arrived at his border—and he wants me to go over there and curse them so that he can battle them successfully."

What a whitewash job *that* was! A vast horde of people from Egypt indeed. They were Israelites and Balaam jolly well knew it. And he knew that Balak was their enemy.

God's answer was brief and to the point. "Don't do it," He said. "You are not to curse them, for I have blessed them."

Well, that was that. If God had blessed them, then indeed no amount of cursing would do any good, and Balaam knew it. The thing to do of course would be to go right downstairs in the morning and tell the messengers so.

*To make them look different than they really are.

22

But Balak was a rich king. It was a shame to let such an opportunity go by . . .

"I Sorta Have to Say No"

Now here's where you begin to wobble.

Instead of coming right out and saying, "No, I can't do it—" the best you can come up with is a halfhearted, "Well, I sorta have to say no." But you don't mean it. And the people you say it to, *know* you don't mean it. Actually what you're saying is, "I sorta have to say no. But I'd really like to do it."

And so you've left the door open, which is always a bad idea when you've left temptation lurking outside.

This is what Balaam did. The next morning, he told the men, "You'll have to run along home. The Lord won't let me do it." But they knew he wanted to. And he *knew* they knew he wanted to. It was such a wishy-washy refusal that the door was wide open for them to come back and try again.

"But the Temptation Is Bigger Than Ever"

Of course it is. If you'd strangled it in the first place, it wouldn't be around to plague* you any more. Instead of that, you've put it just outside the door. But you keep sneaking out there with goodies to feed it. So it's alive and healthy.

This is what Balaam did, so of course it was only a matter of time when the messengers came back. And this time with a bigger and better offer. There were more of them, to begin with, and they were a more distinguished group of ambassadors than the first ones had been. "King Balak *pleads* with you to come!" they cried. "He promises you

---

*It wouldn't be around to pester you.

23

great honors and any payment you ask. Name your own figure. Only come and curse these people for us!"

Ahhhh. Now they were talking money. Balaam's beady eyes bounced in his head. He began to think. And he thought BIG. "Ahh," he told them, "If King Balak were to give me a palace filled with silver and gold, I still couldn't go against the commandment of the Lord my God."

"Hmmmmmm, I'll Ask Again"

What do you mean, you'll ask again? Are you still bothering the Lord about this? Trying to get Him to change His mind? You *know* it's wrong. He's already told you. If you intend to do it anyway, asking Him about it is like robbing a bank and then having a word of prayer in the getaway car. Whom do you think you are kidding?

Balaam did this. Now that he had planted the idea in their minds that he was thinking big, he came out with the rest of it. "However,"* he said, "tarry here for the night. My servants will put you up. And I'll ask the Lord again to see if He has anything to add to what He has already said."

Well now the door was open, with the hinges off. He had practically invited the temptation in for a snack and a Coke.

"You Mean I Have a Choice?"

Of course, you have a choice. God doesn't tie up your hands and tape up your mouth to keep you from doing and saying the wrong things. He doesn't keep you locked up to make you obey. He gave you a mind of your own.**

"Go ahead," God told Balaam. "But I have already told you you could not curse them. For I have blessed them. But

---

*Oh, oh, here we go again.
**But your bad choices grieve Him, and don't you forget it.

watch your tongue, Balaam. One wrong word out of you, and you'll have *Me* to answer to."

Now Balaam should have quit while he was ahead. It was plainer than ever that what he was about to do, was wrong. He should have had the sense to know it. But the possibility of all those riches was dangling in front of him, like a carrot in front of a rabbit.

He made his choice.

The next morning, he had his donkey saddled* and started out with his two servants and the ambassadors on the long trek to King Balak.

"I Chose. But Now My Conscience Is Pinging"

Well, God isn't through with you, after you've made the wrong choice. For He loves you with an everlasting love. And He's not about to let you get in trouble so easily. He'll speak to you in a dozen different ways—through your parents, through your teachers and through your friends.** And if you're dead set on what it is that you want to do, you're not going to like any of it. And things will happen that will get in your way. God will see to that. All sorts of pesky little things. And they will seem accidental. But you'd better believe they are not. It is still God speaking to you— "Hold it. Don't rush into this thing!"

But of all the strange ways God ever spoke to anyone, the strangest is the way He spoke to Balaam.

Balaam trekked along with the VIP's from Balak, and his own two servants.

Did he intend to obey the Lord?

He did not.

He still had his own plan in the back of his mind. He was

---

*In those days, instead of saying "Bring the car around," they said "Bring the donkey around."

Your **real friends—the ones who are obeying the Lord.

25

still hoping he could win the Lord over to his own way of thinking.

And that was when the "pinging" began.

That was when God began to speak to Balaam, and in the strangest way you could imagine.

He was riding along with his two servants. He had made his choice. And everything seemed to be going his way, quite comfortably. When suddenly—

His donkey stopped short, as if she'd been startled by something. Then she bolted off the road into a field! Balaam looked around to see what could have frightened her. There was nothing, nobody in sight. So he beat her back onto the road again. And they proceeded on their journey. Strange, Balaam thought. She'd never done anything like that before. Why, she acted as though she'd *seen* something.

Ah, well. It was nothing to worry about, he thought, as the road got narrower and went between two vineyard walls. He gave her a little nudge to edge her on through. It was noth—

Wait a minute. The donkey began to hedge. She veered to the side, for all the world as though she'd seen something again! Something—or *someone*—standing there! She squirmed past whatever or *who*ever she thought she saw, and pressed against the wall—

Ouch!

She pressed against the wall so hard, Balaam's foot was scraped and crushed in the process.

"Ouch!" he bellowed aloud. "Watch where you're going, you—you *jackass!*" And he beat the poor donkey again. This time he was furious!

He was still muttering to both the donkey and himself, when they got to a *very* narrow spot in the road, and the donkey stopped again. And again she acted as though she saw somebody!

And then without any warning, she just lay down in the road, toppling Balaam with her!

Balaam scrambled to his feet in a fit of rage, crushed foot and all. And he beat her again with his staff. And then—

"What have I done? What have I *ever* done to you that you should beat me like this? Three times!"

What???

Who said that? *Good grief.* It was the donkey! She was talking!

For a moment Balaam forgot she was only a donkey. He talked right back to her!

"You've made me look like a fool!" he sputtered. "I wish I had a sword with me. If I had a sword with me, I'd kill you!"

They stood there, glaring at each other.

"Have I ever done anything like this before in my entire life?" the donkey asked. And Balaam sighed. This was all so completely bewildering he could hardly believe it was happening.

"No," he finally said. "You've never done anything like this before."

And then the Lord finally opened Balaam's eyes.

Standing there in the roadway was an angel with a drawn sword! The donkey *had* seen someone!

Balaam did what anyone would do in such circumstances. He fell flat on the ground.

"Okay, Okay, I Won't Do It!"

If God puts enough clanging warnings in your way, you might come to this conclusion. And turn back from whatever it was you were about to do. Happy are you, if you do this. It's better to listen to the warnings and quit while you're ahead, than to go stubbornly on—and learn the hard way.

Balaam's warning was clanging, loud and clear. "Why did you beat your donkey those three times?" the angel demanded. "I've come to stop you because you're headed for trouble. Three times your donkey saw me and shied away from me. Otherwise you might have been killed."

Well, Balaam was frightened nearly out of his wits. "I didn't realize you were there," he said. "I'm wrong, I'm wrong. I'll go back home if you don't want me to go on."

Now it looks as though the Lord was giving Balaam a chance to mend his ways. But the angel said to him, "No. Go ahead if you have a mind to. Go on with the men. But you can only say what I tell you to say."

"Yes, yes. Anything you say," muttered Balaam, scrambling to his feet, and glad to be getting let off so lightly. Why he'd nearly been killed! Phew!

So he decided to obey. Not because he loved God. But because he was scared to death.

"I've Decided to Do Right"

When you say this, you'd better mean it. And if you don't mean it, you'd better duck. There is nothing worse than "going through the motions" of being good, when you don't really mean it. There is nothing worse than being a *phony*.

Well, Balaam went on his journey. He had decided to do right. But it was only because there didn't seem to be any other way for him to go. He was "going through the motions." And from there on out, he went through the motions in grand style.

Talk about royal receptions!

When King Balak heard Balaam was in the way, he left his capital and went out to meet him at the border of his land.

"Why did you delay so long?" he cried. "Didn't you believe me when I said I would give you great honors?"

"Well," said Balaam, "I'm here. But I have no power to say anything except what God tells me to say."

He didn't tell King Balak that God had told him he could *not* curse the Israelites.

Cagey rascal!

The next morning King Balak took Balaam to a mountain-top that had an excellent view of the entire Israelite camp.* And with much huffing and puffing, Balaam ordered King Balak to have seven altars built and to prepare seven young bulls and seven rams for sacrifice. King Balak followed the orders and the altars were built and the sacrifices were burnt.

Pronto.

Then Balaam said, "Stay here by your burnt offerings. And I'll go see if the Lord will meet me. I'll tell you what He says."

And Balaam went a short distance aside, and spoke to the Lord. And got his instructions. And when he came back, the news was all bad.

"How can I curse what God has not cursed?" he said. "These Israelites live by themselves—they're separate from any other nation. And they're as numerous as dust. There are so many of them, you couldn't count them all."

There was a silence. Then, "What have you *done* to me?" demanded King Balak. "I told you to curse them. Now you've *blessed* them!"

Clearly, they were off to a bad start.

"Come with me to another place," King Balak said. "From there you can't see the whole camp. You can only see a *part* of the camp. You can curse at least *that* many. And he took Balaam to another mountaintop.**

And with more huffing and puffing, Balaam ordered the altars and sacrifices again. And told King Balak to stand by his burnt offerings. And went off to meet the Lord.

The news was as bad as ever.

"God is not a man that He could lie," he told King Balak when he came back. "He doesn't change His mind like

*Mount Bamoth-baal.
**Mount Pisgah.

29

people do. Look, He told me to bless them for *He* had blessed them," he finished lamely. "So I have to bless them."

Good grief.

"If you aren't going to curse them, at least don't bless them!" Balak said in desperation. Then he sighed. "We'll try another place," he said. "Maybe it will please your God to curse them from there."

So they made another try. This time to the top of Mount Peor. Here they could see only the tail end of the camp. Maybe *this* would do it.

More huffing and puffing. More altars. More burnt sacrifices. By this time, Balaam knew he was licked. God planned to bless Israel, come what may. He didn't go apart to meet the Lord this time. But he knew the answer. There was nothing he could do but bless them again.

By this time King Balak was purple. "I called you to curse my enemies and instead you've blessed them!" he shouted, striking his hands together. "Three times!" he bellowed. "Get out of here!"

"Go home! Go back to your home! I had planned to promote you to great honor. But God has kept you from it."

Then Balaam reached the height of his spiritual phoniness.* "Didn't I tell your messengers," he said piously, "that even if you gave me a palace filled with silver and gold, I could say only what God told me to say?" And he sighed a pious sigh, and said, "Yes. I shall return now to my own home."

What a great man! What a tower of strength! What a man of God! All out for the Lord, there, and no mistake. Except for one thing.

"But I Don't Really Mean It"

And so Balaam, after having done a great job, went home.

*He had a trick up his sleeve.

30

Sounds terrific, doesn't it?

Great show!

It's a great show he put on—while everyone was looking.

There was another little show going on in private—while no one was looking. It was when Balaam and Balak were finally alone.*

"Psssssst," said Balaam.

"What's this?" said Balak.

"I couldn't get God to curse them," said Balaam. "I really couldn't. You know that. God loves those people. And I could not turn Him away from them. *But—*"

"Yes?" said King Balak. "But what?"

"But," said Balaam, "nobody said anything about turning *them* away from *Him*."

"But how?" said Balak. "How?"

"Easy," said Balaam. "Tempt them to sin. Now here's what I would advise you to do."

"I'm listening," said King Balak.

And Balaam proceeded to outline the most diabolical** scheme you could ever imagine. "It was guaranteed," said Balaam, "to make Israel fall on her face." And he probably had his hand out when he said it. There is no doubt but that he got the reward that he'd been wanting so long.

And the scheme?

Simple.

Just get the Israelites to run around with the wrong crowd—namely, King Balak's very own people.

Get them to go out with each other. Hang around with each other. Visit each other. It wouldn't be long before they'd be marrying each other. And it would be only a question of time before the Israelites started worshiping the idols of Balak's people—and—God would soon be out of their minds, and out of their hearts.

*Either then or on a later visit. We don't know.

**Straight from the devil.

Yes, indeed. It was an evil plan.

And what is worse—it worked.

So many of the Israelites became idol worshipers, that God finally said to Moses, "Take up arms against these people for leading you into idolatry!"

So a great battle was fought, accompanied by the Ark of God, and the trumpets blaring. And the enemy was defeated.*

Well, the Bible tells us how Balaam wound up. In one short sentence.

"Balaam, the son of Beor, was also killed."**

Balaam got the reward he wanted so badly. There was only one problem. He didn't live very long to enjoy it.

And all through the Bible, the writers kept bringing him up as a horrible example of what not to do. Of what a hero should *not* be.***

What About You?

Do you have some "buts" in your life? Are you a "Sunday" Christian? Do you have an "everyday" life and a "Sunday" life?

God warned Balaam again and again and *again*.

First he gave him a gentle nudge (The donkey bolted off the road). Then He clobbered him. (The donkey made him crush his foot against the wall.) Then He stopped him in his tracks. (The donkey lay down and would go no farther.)

Now when Balaam got his foot crushed, he should have gone home and soaked it, and forgotten the whole nasty business. But he didn't.

And he went on and on and *on*—until it was too late.

What about you?

*Numbers 31:1-8.
**Numbers 31:8
***II Peter 2:15; Jude 11; Revelation 2:14

4

The Man Who Didn't
Have a Funeral

Exodus 1—13; 32; Deuteronomy 32:48-52; 34

"I'll Never Make the Hall of Fame"

"Some people manage to do such great things with their lives that everybody remembers them, even long after they've gone. Some of them even 'lie in state' and then they're trundled around to a lot of states where people line the streets to see them go by before they're put in a VIP place where everybody goes to visit them for years and years, and kids study about them in history books.

"If I live seventy years that seems like forever, but when you put it in days, why it's only 25,567 days,* and that doesn't seem long enough to do anything great or even anything small for that matter. 25,567 days. Phew! How many days have I spent already and I haven't even got started? I don't even have time for basketball practice and homework and all my clubs.

"I guess to make the Hall of Fame or go down in history you'd have to be at least a great athlete, or better still a great statesman. When great statesmen die, why the whole

*Yes, leap year is figured in here.

world knows about it. And they put flags at half-mast and everything."

Well, lying in state or having a tomb everybody visits and that gets on exams is a great thing indeed.* So great, in fact, that some men spend their lives struggling to attain it. Ancient kings practically spent their reigns building their tombs and furnishing them with untold wealth. But there was a great statesman once, who not only didn't have a tomb—he didn't have a funeral. In fact he didn't even have a grave.

It was Moses.

"What? Moses?!?"

"Moses a statesman? I always thought of Moses as a man of God. I never thought of him as a statesman."

Well, let's define our terms. *Statesman: A man who exhibits great wisdom and ability in directing the affairs of a government or in dealing with important public issues.*

Moses was all of that, all right. He had the wisdom of God.

He was not only a great man of God; he was one of the greatest statesmen who ever lived. That wasn't the way he'd planned it. But that was the way it turned out.

He Was Off to a Bad Start

He started out in life condemned to death, before he was old enough to stand up and defend himself, or indeed even old enough to hear the verdict.

He was only an infant.

Which would have been dandy except that he happened to be an Israelite infant. And in those days that wasn't exactly a healthy thing to be. The Israelites were slaves in

*Even if it's only part of a 10-part question.

36

Egypt under the rule of a very cruel Pharaoh. And when Pharaoh decreed that every Israelite baby boy be killed, Moses' wings were about to be clipped before he had a chance to grow any feathers.

But his mother made a basket* and smeared it with tar so it wouldn't leak and put it in the Nile, and left his sister Miriam to stay and watch. And who should find it but one of the handmaidens of the Pharaoh's daughter. And who should adopt the baby but the Pharoah's daughter herself. So in a twinkling of an eye, Moses went from being condemned to death, to being a prince!

And he grew up with no problems whatever except to acquire a fantastic education, and learn not to trip over his royal mantle.

Now he could have had a tomb as splendid as a palace with no trouble at all, loaded with everything from jewelry to golden chariots. He was headed for a life of incredible glamour and riches and fame.

But something got in the way.

Home Is Where the Heart Is

It was his great statesman's heart. He wouldn't have defined it as such because the term "statesman" hadn't been invented yet. But his heart somehow got tangled up with the Israelite slaves who were being so cruelly treated by the Pharaoh. And the Israelite slaves were of course his own people.

He killed an Egyptian slave driver who was whipping one of the slaves.

And fled for his own life.

And went to Midian, off in the desert near Mount Sinai. And wound up living there and tending sheep. So again, in a twinkling of an eye, so to speak, he went from being a

*They called it an "ark."

37

prince to being an absolute nobody. He was a nobody for 14,610 days. Which doesn't seem long until you stop to think that it's forty years.

Then God called him* to lead his people out of Egypt.

"From Nobody to Leader Again?"

Yes, from nobody to leader again. In the twinkling of an eye.

Of course he gave the usual excuses to God:

"But I'm not the person for a big job like that!" (Exod. 3:11).

"They won't do what *I* tell them to!" (Exod. 4:1).

"I'm just not a good speaker! I never have been! (Exod. 4:10).

"Lord, please! Send somebody else!" (Exod. 4:13).

It would seem that forty years in the wilderness had certainly taken the ginger out of him. But actually it had taken out of him all confidence in wealth or in power—or in everything, in fact, except God.

When God said, "I'll be with you," Moses went. God told him to take his brother Aaron with him, and they packed their duffle bags and marched into one of the most well-known stories in history. It sounds like a story but it actually happened.

Moses marched in to Pharaoh and demanded that he let the Israelites go.

Ten plagues, two refusals, three compromises, two stalemates, one change-of-mind and one "yes" later, Pharoah did.**

They wandered around in circles in the wilderness, until at last, pretty well baked and sandblasted,*** they had

*God spoke to him from the burning bush. Remember?
**You can read about it in Exodus 4—12.
*** The wind and the sandstorms in the desert were fierce!

learned their lessons and were ready to enter the Promised Land.

"But When Was Moses a Statesman?"

"Everything he did was so dramatic—he sounds more like a miracle worker than a statesman. He did everything with such dash and derring-do."

Yes. But hidden under all the dash and all the drama is another story of Moses.

Moses the statesman.

There was the time when he went up into Mount Sinai to receive the Ten Commandments from God, and while he was gone, the Israelites made themselves a golden calf and proceeded to worship it.

And God said, "I'll destroy them!"

And then God said something that, had Moses been a mere politician, he would have taken Him up on it at once.

"I'll destroy them—and I will make *you,* Moses, into a great nation *instead of them!*"

But Moses begged God not to do it! "Lord," he pleaded, "Why is Your anger so hot against Your people?" And, "Do You want the Egyptians to say You delivered them from Egypt only to destroy them?" And, "Remember Your promise to Your people!"

When Moses got down from the mountain and saw the golden calf for himself, he went back up into the mountain again. "Lord," he begged, "these people have sinned a great sin. Yet now if You will only forgive their sin—"

And then Moses made one of the most amazing statements in the whole Bible. "If not—" he said, *"then blot ME out of the book You have written."*

Now no human leader ever showed such love for his people as that. That is better than good, greater than brave, bigger than life!

And later, much, much later, when they were at Kadesh,

39

right on the border of the Promised Land, and they were wailing and wishing they were dead—Moses saved their skin again. It was right after the spies' gloomy report about the Promised Land, and before Moses finally lost his temper and whammed that rock.

The Lord said it again. "I will disinherit them and destroy them and make *you* into a nation far greater and mightier than they are!"

Now Moses was pretty weary by this time—weary of their groanings and weary of their stubbornness and weary of the very sight of them.

Here was a chance to get rid of them forever.

And be made leader of a mightier nation.

And have the Lord on his side!

What an offer for a very discouraged man to mull over!

But Moses didn't mull. Not for a moment. "Lord," he said, "*Everybody* knows You lead and protect these people day and night. Now if You give up on them, everyone will say that You just weren't strong enough to bring them into the Promised Land. I *plead with You* to forgive them, just as You've forgiven them all the time since we left Egypt until now!"

Yes. Every weary, glum, complaining step of the way.

And the Lord said, "All right. I'll pardon them as you requested."

And there went the last chance of any fame or power for Moses, gone with the desert wind.

Now *that's a statesman.*

"But Everything Was Going His Way!"

"I don't mean to put Moses down, but after all, it's easy to be noble and generous when you're sure of your power. I mean Moses knew that he was the boss and nobody was going to take his power away, no matter what happened. I can be president of my class and I can have all kinds of problems and still keep my cool. But if somebody else got put in my place, then I think I might come all unpasted. What if Moses' power got taken away—poof—just like that? Would he be so noble then? I mean would his thoughts still be about his people? Or about himself?"

"What-would-you-do-if?" is a good question. And Moses had a chance to find out the answer.

One day the Lord said to Moses, "Go up into Mount Abarim and look across the river to the land I have given to the people of Israel. After you have seen it, you shall die. For you did not obey me in Kadesh."*

And Moses didn't say, "Lord, whoever can take my place?" Or, "How can these people ever do without me?" or, "What? Somebody else in *my* position?" Or even, "All right, Lord. I'd better appoint a successor. I have just the man in mind. Of course, somebody of *my* choice will be best; I know the problems and I can train him."

No.

"Lord," he said, "please appoint a new leader for the people, a man who will lead them into battle and care for them."

Moses not only didn't quibble; he left the choice of a leader with God.

And the Lord said, "Go get Joshua,** and as all the people watch, charge him with the responsibility of leading the people."

And Moses did as the Lord commanded.

Which answers the "what-if" question.

No—He Was Going GOD'S Way.

Moses was really counting his life in days now. And there was no time to waste. He got his records up to date. He took

---

*That was the rock-whamming incident.
**More about him later.

care of all his unfinished business. He talked with the people and gave them a rundown on all the things God had told them. He finished writing the accounts of their adventures with God, and gave the writing to the Levite priests. Everything was finished. The time had come.

The Man Who Didn't Have a Funeral

"Go to Mount Nebo in the Abarim mountains," the Lord told Moses, "and climb to its heights."

It must have been a solemn moment when Moses began his journey. The people he had loved stood silent, a vast multitude of them, stretching way back as far as eye could see. He said good-by to his personal officers and close friends. He charged Joshua to be faithful and brave, and they must have embraced each other there, their robes rippling in the desert wind. Then he turned, and with strong sure steps, started up the mountain. He was 120 years old, but his eyesight was perfect, the Bible tells us, and he was still as strong as a young man.

Up, up, he climbed, and the sea of faces grew more distant until they were finally out of sight, and he was climbing alone.

He was going to meet God at last!

At the top, he stood and looked at the breath-taking sweep of the land below. He saw the River Jordan threading its way to the Dead Sea. And the olive trees and the walled cities nestled against the mountains or standing on the plains. There it was, stretching out to the Mediterranean Sea. It was a good land, fertile, and "flowing with milk and honey" as God had said.

There on top of the mountain, he had his last talk with God on earth, and there he died.

The Lord buried him, but no one has ever known the exact place.

The greatest statesman the world has ever known, didn't even have a funeral.

"But Wasn't This His Punishment?"

"God didn't let him go over to the Promised Land. And he didn't even have a funeral. Wasn't that punishment?"

Yes, we'd have to say that was punishment because God definitely told Moses it was. "You can't go over," God said, "because you disobeyed Me."

But if God was punishing Moses, He was punishing with Tender Loving Care. And it did not diminish* Moses' greatness one single whit. For Moses went into God's presence in private and he was buried by God in secret. And there is something very special and precious about this.

"Was That the Last of Moses?"

Many years went by and the great nation of Israel was built and men lived their lives and died, and their children, and their children, and *their* children—

And then God sent Jesus Himself to live on earth.

Now all of this would not be a part of our story here. Except for one thing.

One day Jesus went up to Mount Hermon with three of His disciples to pray. And the disciples fell asleep. And suddenly—

All nature seemed to stand still. A great hush fell on the birds, on the trees, on the insects. Not a thing stirred. It was as if creation in that little spot had stopped in adoration. And the disciples looked at Jesus in wonder.

His face was changing! It was becoming radiant with light—and His garments were blazing with light, like the sun itself! And then—

*Make it any less.

Two men appeared in heavenly splendor and majesty. The Bible says, "Then two men appeared and began talking with Jesus. They were splendid in appearance, glorious to see; and they were speaking of His death at Jerusalem, to be carried out in accordance with God's plan."

Then a bright cloud came down and the disciples watched, frightened, as Jesus and the two men disappeared into it. Then, out of the cloud, a voice. "This is My beloved Son. Listen to Him!"

The very voice of God!

The disciples fell to the ground in terror.

Then everything was quiet, quiet. And someone touched them on their shoulders. When they looked up, it was Jesus. He was alone. "Get up," He said simply, "don't be afraid."

It was a shattering experience.

They didn't tell anyone for a long, long time that they had seen Jesus radiant with light. And the two men in heavenly splendor and majesty. Or that one of the men had been Elijah.

And the other one had been Moses.

There's More to Being a Hero Than Derring-do

It's great to be a dashing hero. It's great to go down in history. It's great to make the Hall of Fame. But Moses did the greatest thing of all.

He was more concerned with others than he was for himself. And, except for one mistake, he was completely obedient to God. "There has never been another prophet like Moses," the Bible says, "for the Lord talked to him face to face."*

He was a great Christian statesman.

*Deuteronomy 34:10 (TLB)

44

What About You?

Now you might not work your way up to a fancy tomb. But God just might have you in mind to be one of His great Christian statesmen.*

That may not be the way you planned it, but it could be the way it will turn out.

"Who says I can?"

Well, who says you *can't?*

*Or woman!

5
The Dust-Eater

Numbers 27:12-23; Deuteronomy 34; Joshua 1:1-18

"I'm Just out of the Running"

"I've been a second-stringer for so long, I've given up ever being able to accomplish anything. I seldom even get a *chance*. If I went in for athletics I'd always be on the bench. If I got in the game, I'd be at the bottom if the heap. If I ran in a race I'd eat the other kids' dust. If I competed for an office or in a test, I'd come out second-best. If I sat in a committee meeting, I'd take a back seat. If I were written in a story, I'd never be the hero; I'd be his faithful companion. If I were a part of a letter, I'd be the P.S. I'm just one of those nothing-to-brag-about, nothing-to-write-home-about kids.

"Just call me ole 'Dust-Eater.'"

"What am I doing *wrong?*"

Everybody feels like this at some time in his life. Of course, *all* of these things are not true of you. Or even *most* of them. Trouble is, when even *one* of them is true, instead of realizing that it is probably only temporary, you think it's going to be a way of life for you.

And it simply isn't so.

It Happens to Some of the Best People

There was a man, once, who must have felt this way, at least *some* of the time. This man's name was Joshua. And he played second fiddle to, of all people—*Moses*.

Now Moses was so first-rate that all by himself he was a majority. He could outshine, outstrip, outrank and outflank anybody, single-handed.

Moses was the great one. He was the superman. When they walked outside, Joshua was in his shadow. When they were in the Tabernacle, Joshua couldn't hold a candle to him. When they climbed a mountain, Joshua was left behind in the dust.

"Without a Good Background You Don't Have a Chance!"

Well, Joshua was born a slave. He was born a slave in Egypt, the son of a certain unknown man named Nun, of the tribe of Ephraim. And he grew up a slave, while Moses was living in the desert.

The Pharaoh was building a huge temple,* bigger and more glorious than any yet built in Egypt. The slaves worked in the Nile Delta, under the blazing sun. There were slave drivers to see that they worked and to beat them if they faltered.

Joshua was probably dragging a hoe through mud to mix the straw in for bricks when Moses returned and faced Pharaoh and cried, "Let my people go!"

When Pharaoh said, "And who is God, that I should obey His voice and let the Israelites go?"—Joshua was one of those Isarelites.

And when Pharaoh cried out, "I am Pharaoh! I answer to no one. These people are my slaves. Why do you keep them from doing their work? If they do not have enough to keep

*As a memorial to himself, naturally.

48

them busy, I'll give them more!"—Joshua was one of those whose work was doubled.

And when Pharaoh bellowed, "Ye are idle, ye are idle! It is because ye are idle that ye ask to go on journeys to worship your God. Work! And you'll have no time for journeys!"—Joshua was one of the hopeless ones.

Joshua had a background all right—all negative. He didn't have a thing going for him.

If he'd been part of a letter, he'd have been the P.S.

"What Kind of People Do You Admire?"

There was a picture of a boy in one of our large city papers. He looked very odd. Very alone and bewildered and empty. Who was he, the paper wanted to know. He had no identification.

Somewhere along the way, he had admired the wrong people and got into the wrong crowd, and made the wrong choices. And he'd got more and more tangled in his own choices and in his own sin until now there was no way back. For the picture of him had been taken in the morgue. He had been found dead on somebody's lawn, tossed there from a passing car, a casualty of a gang war.

Whom do you admire? Whom do you run after? What kind of people do you like to be with? It's a good idea to stop and take stock every once in awhile. For the person—or the crowd—you chase after and like to be with, could jolly well determine what kind of person you finally are going to be.

When Pharaoh finally let the Israelites go, and, led by Moses, they started their weary trek across the wilderness—Joshua was there too.

Now he could have gone in any direction. He was a lad with a whole future before him and all sorts of choices to make. He could have joined a crowd of grumblers. Or he could have hung out with a crowd of lazy sluggards whose main goal in life was to get out of as much work and as much responsibility as possible. Or he could have joined a crowd of scoffers-at-authority. Or he could have been a "loner," trudging along, sulking—not wanting to speak to or be with anybody. But he chased after Moses, he wanted to be with Moses, he was happy when he was with Moses, he liked to listen to Moses.

Joshua admired a good man.

Now you don't have to admire and chase after the out-and-out wicked to get off the track. Just joining a group of grumblers will do very nicely, for a start.

You Have to Follow Before You Can Lead

Now this is a difficult subject to get straightened out, for it's a subject on which adults seem to speak with a forked tongue. Out of one side of the mouth they tell you that you have to sit back, listen and learn, before you can take responsibility and be a leader. And out of the other side of the mouth they tell you to get going, give yourself a push, take yourself by the scruff of the neck, be more aggressive, jump into the fray, and, in short, "get with it."

It's sort of like being caught in cross-currents. You don't know which way to swim—it leaves you bobbing up and down with indecision.

What to be—the leader? Or the faithful companion?

It isn't really so difficult, for actually there is a bit of truth on both sides. You do have to follow, to learn, to be willing to take orders. But you also have to be ready to take responsibility when it's dumped in your lap. And there are times when you *do* have to jump into the fray.

Frank Ryan of the Cleveland Browns knows how to run with the ball and fake the other guys out if their undergarments. He knows about geometric function theory and linear transformations, complex variable and Cauchy sequences.*

BUT—

"The process of becoming a skilled pro quarterback," says Ryan, "is a process of being thrown into the fray and having to live or die in it. It's a process of learning, and the only way you can learn is to be out there under game conditions."

If it seems to you that responsibility has been dumped into your lap and you're not prepared for it, stop and think. You may find that here and there, in this situation and that, you had, after all, picked up a bit of know-how and experience. And that God had been preparing you for this for a long time.

You were more ready than you thought!

Things that happened to you didn't seem important at the time, but with God nothing happens by accident. You were learning from each experience whether you realized it or not.

After you become a leader, life is one astonishment after another. "How did I know this?" you think. And then you realize that you have known "this" for a long time.

And you remember way back when you learned it.

Joshua probably didn't fully realize what God was preparing him for when he was listening to, and learning from, Moses. Being free was a pretty heady business. Every day was a new adventure. He knew he had to be ready for anything that came.

"Anything" happened sooner than he expected.

They were out in the wilderness only a couple of months when,

"Attack! Enemy attack!"

What's this? Was somebody fooling?

*What? You don't know these football terms? Ask your dad when he's watching a game on TV some Saturday. Ask him during the commercials, though.

No. It was the Amalekites, and they weren't fooling.*
Call to arms!

Moses appointed a leader to gather the fighting men and go to war against them.

The leader was Joshua. And he was ready.

And with Moses' prayers and God's help, he licked them, too.

Which made him the "man of the hour."

Which could have made him quite cocky. A thing like that could give a fellow the feeling that he had arrived.

But what do we hear that Joshua did after this?

He waited on Moses. He was Moses' right-hand man. He ran his errands. He stayed in the shadow.

And he kept on learning.

When Moses went into the Tabernacle, Joshua was with him. When Moses went up to the mountain to talk with God and get the Ten Commandments, Joshua went with him. And waited at a distance, while Moses went alone to talk to God.

Joshua was always behind.

The faithful companion.

The Dust-Eater.

Two years later, when they reached the borders of the Promised Land, Moses sent twelve spies in to look over the land and bring back a report. Twelve hand-picked men.

One of them was Joshua.

You know the story. Ten of the spies came back shaken out of their sandals. "We can't take them!" they cried. "They're like giants! And their cities are walled! They'll crush us to a pulp!"

"Ohhh," the people wailed, and "Auuuuuuugh!"

But two of the spies cried, "Hold it! It's a wonderful

*These warlike bandits had been pestering God's people since the days of Abraham.

country! And the Lord loves us. He will bring us safely into the land! Don't be afraid of them!"

One of them was Joshua.

And forty years later, when God told Moses that his work was ended, there was no doubt that a new leader had to be appointed. There was no doubt that this leader had to be absolutely tops. And there was no doubt who this leader would be. God's instructions were very plain.

"Go get Joshua."

So the man who had a background that was all negative, who had nothing going for him, who was always behind— the faithful companion, the dust-eater—became the leader of the whole Israelite nation.

Joshua was on his way.

The Choice Is Yours

He couldn't help his background. But he *could* help his choices. And he chose to listen and learn. He admired a great man. He was willing to follow. And when the time came, he was ready to lead.

And oh, how close to God he kept! God summed it all up when He instructed Moses. "Go get Joshua," He said, *"who has My Spirit in him."*

Your background is a combination of your origin and your education and your experience. You are the sum total of all three. You can't help your origin. But you *can* help your choices.

6

Will the God of Moses Be with Me?

Joshua 3 and 4

It's a Hard Act to Follow!

"I'd hate to be class president after *him!*"

Have you ever felt this way about somebody you know who's a leader? "He's so popular and so smart and everybody looks up to him. He doesn't have any trouble getting other people to do what he wants. I don't think I could ever get people to follow me like that. I'd sure hate to have to step into his shoes. I don't think I could handle it."

Joshua must have felt that way. Imagine having to follow Moses! What big shoes to fill! What a hard act to follow! Joshua had lived in the shadow of a leader for way over forty years. And now suddenly, out of the blue, he *was* the leader.

"But Those Men Had God!"

"People like Moses and Joshua didn't have anything to worry about. They had a direct connection with God. I .mean, He said, 'Jump,' and they said, 'How high?' And that's all there was to it. I can't believe that God would ever be that close to me. Sometimes I feel like He doesn't even know I'm here."

Well, Joshua must have felt that way too. About Moses, that is. "Dear Lord," he must have thought. "I've never had the closeness to you that Moses had. There was never any doubt in people's minds that You were giving him his orders. He never had to prove anything. You proved everything for him. I love You, Lord, and I trust You—but there are times when I just feel squeamish and my stomach flops and my heart fails and I can't help but wonder: Will the God of Moses be with me? If I could only know. If I could only—just once—really know."

"Oh, Come On"

"Joshua was never squeamish.* Everybody who knows anything about the Bible knows about the fantastic things he did. Why, he was one of the giants of the Old Testament. Joshua? Squeamish? I can't believe it. After all, didn't God talk to him the same as He talked to Moses?"

Well, Joshua did feel squeamish, and you'd better believe it. And yes, God did talk to him as He had talked to Moses. And one of the very first things God talked to him about was his *squeamishness*. For God kept repeating one thought, over and over and over again.

"You are the new leader," God said, "and I will not fail to help you."

And then He said, "Be strong and brave."

"You will be a successful leader."

And then He said, "Be strong and courageous."

"You must obey the laws Moses gave you," God said, "and see that the people do too."

And then He said, "Be bold and strong!"

*Your stomach gets tied in knots easily.

56

"I am with you," God said, "wherever you go."
And then He said, "Banish fear and doubt!"

So you can see that anyone who has to be told to be brave
four times in one conversation, must be a bit squeamish.

"I'm Ready to Go"

"I have my marching orders. I know what I'm supposed
to do. I have it right from the Word of God. But I'm still not
sure how God is going to work this out. I have my instructions; I just wish He had told me *more*."

Well, Joshua had his marching orders too. And he passed
God's instructions on to the people. But he had no positive
proof that God was going to do what He said He would do.
He told the people to get ready to cross the Jordan River.
"In three days," he told them, "we will go across and con-
quer and live in the land which God has given us!"

Now *that* was a strong statement!

And he sent two spies ahead to find a spot in the Jordan
where they could cross, and to go over the Jordan and spy
out Jericho. And come back and give him a report.

Jericho was the first city that had to be conquered in the
Promised Land.

"It's Hard to Wait, Lord"

"Sometimes I wish what I had to do, I could just hurry up
and *do*. It's hard to wait to see just how You're going to
work it out."

Yes.

It's fun to read suspense stories. And the reason why
they're called suspense stories is that you have to wait and
see what's going to happen. And sometimes you don't know
until the last minute just how it's going to turn out. When
it's a story it's fun. But when you're living it and have to
wait to see what's going to happen—

And wait—and wait—and wait—
It isn't such fun.

It's while you're waiting that you can get squeamish again.

It must have been hard for Joshua to wait for the spies to get back and hear what they had to say. And he must have thought of that time, more than forty years ago, when *he'd* been sent over as a spy by Moses.* He'd been sent over with eleven other spies. And only he and Caleb had come back with the report to "go ahead!" Being brave had been lonely business. And now, after forty years, being brave was still lonely business.

All Signals Say Go!

This is when it's *really* hard to wait!

The spies** came back from Jericho with good news. The people in Jericho had heard about the Israelites. They knew they were coming. They knew of the fantastic victories God had given them. They were all scared to death. God had absolutely paralyzed them with fear.

Everything was all set.

The signal was Go-go-go!

Joshua ordered the people to break up camp and leave Acacia, and travel to the edge of the Jordan.

"But Why Now?"

"At first I was in a hurry, but now I'm beginning to change my mind. I'll do whatever you say, Lord, but why do I have to do it *now?* Everything is so mixed up right now —there couldn't be a worse time to do this. If I could just

*Chapter 1
**You'll find out about their adventures there, in the next chapter.

wait until things quiet down, it would be easier. But really, Lord, right now things are *wild!*"

Things were pretty mixed up for Joshua and the Israelites, too. To begin with, it was the wrong time of the year— Spring.

And the melting snow on the mountaintops sent so many torrential* streams hurtling down the mountainside into the Jordan, that the Jordan didn't know what to do with them all. So the Jordan overflowed its banks. When the Israelites got there, the Jordan was a raging monster! Why ever would God want them to cross it *then?* There were other seasons of the year when it was quiet and sluggish, and there were times of the year when it was quite low. Right now it looked as though it were ready to fight anybody who dared put a foot in it! It almost seemed like something alive —daring them to cross!

Why now, Lord, of all times? Why not wait until things quieted down a bit?

But the Lord had told Joshua: "Go *now.*"

And Joshua *went.*

"But How?"

A step at a time is how. Joshua didn't worry about the step *after* the next step. Or even the next step. He just trusted God for the step he was taking then and there, at the moment. "When you see the priests carrying the Ark of God,** follow them. You have never before been where

*The water poured down like crazy!

**The Ark of God was a chest about 45 inches long, 27 inches wide and 27 inches high, made of acacia wood and covered with pure gold. On each side were two golden rings through which poles could be inserted for carrying it. The lid was made of solid gold and on it were two angels of gold, with outspread wings. And what was inside? Why, the stone tablets with the Ten Commandments on them, a golden pot of manna. And Aaron's rod that budded! It was to remind the Israelites of God's presence.

you're going now. So they will guide you. But stay about a half a mile behind, with a clear space between you and the Ark. And be sure that you don't get any closer. For tomorrow, the Lord will do a great miracle."

Did You Hear Me Lord? How?!?

It was hardly dawn in the huge camp of the Israelites when people began stirring. Everyone had his job to do. Some of them pulled up stakes and did the last-minute packing. Others went out and gathered the manna. It was almost the last time they would have manna. And there was no more pillar of cloud; the Ark of God would guide them from here on out.

Joshua had already given the order to the priests. "Take up the Ark," he'd said, "and lead us across the river." He told them to wait at the edge of the river for further orders. But he had already told them that they were going to get across—they weren't going to stay there!

Then he gave the Israelites their last-minute instructions.

They were ready to go.

"But Things Aren't the Same Anymore!"

"But times change, you know. They aren't the same any more. They aren't the same with me as they were with my parents. Or my grandparents. This is *different*. It's all right to say, have faith—

"But things are like they've never been before!"

Well, everything had changed for Joshua, too. And things were like they'd never been before. Back in Moses' days, he had taken his rod and struck the waters of the Red Sea. And God had caused a strong east wind to blow all night, to hold the waters back. And now, what was this? Joshua was *not* told to strike the water with his rod.

And there wasn't any wind!

It was different than it had ever been before!

But Joshua, without the help of his rod, and without any strong east wind shouted the order. "March!"

The priests hoisted the poles—hup!—up on their shoulders. And started toward the raging waters. If you'd been watching them, you'd have thought they were a suicide squad, going on their last mission to certain death. On and on they marched.

Ten feet away—

Five feet away—

Two feet away—

Then, whoops!

Into the water.

And suddenly—

Up the river a way, the water piled up as though it were up against an invisible dam. The waters below the "dam" went on downstream. Past the Israelites. And out of sight. And no more water came from upstream. The flow of the raging river had actually been held back!

So that, before their very eyes, the raging waters rushed past and were gone—and the river bed was empty!

The priests marched into the river bed until they got to the middle. And there they stopped, holding the Ark, and waited for the people to cross.

And did the people stroll over, gossiping with each other? And talking about the weather? And speculating* on what had happened to the river? And examining the rock formations at the river bottom? And stopping to catch fish flopping in the mud?

They did not!

The Bible tells us they went over in great haste. In other words, they scrambled over as fast as they could, slipping over rocks, breathing hard. It was no time to talk. They went over the way *you* would have gone over, if you

*Trying to guess.

61

thought that any minute the waters would come tumbling downstream again, like a tidal wave!

Hold It a Minute!

After the people were all safely across, Joshua gave orders for twelve men* to get twelve rocks from the center of the river. They did, straining and tugging—and carried them to shore on their shoulders. They were to be taken to Gilgal** to be set up there as a monument, so the Israelites would never forget this incredible*** day.

After the last man had struggled ashore with the huge stone on his shoulder, Joshua shouted to the priests: "Come up from the river bed!"

They came out, slipping and sliding on the rocks, struggling to carry the Ark. The people watched. And as soon as the priests set foot on the other side—

The water that had been held back, way upstream, came tumbling down—roaring, swirling, frothing, raging—to fill the river bed to overflowing!

The Jordan was a raging monster again!

But the Israelites were safe on the other side.

They camped at Gilgal, on the eastern edge of the city of Jericho. And there the twelve stones from the Jordan River were piled up as a monument.

And when the nations west of the Jordan heard about what happened, the Bible tells us their courage melted away completely. They were paralyzed with fear.

Hurry Up and Wait

Well, here they were. Right outside Jericho. But the

*One strong man from each tribe.
**Their next camping place near Jericho.
***Hard to believe.

orders weren't "Charge!" The orders were "Wait." And wait they did, and rested. And celebrated the feast of the Passover. It was on the day after the Passover that the manna stopped coming. The next day they began to eat the provisions of the land about them.

The long weary trek through the wilderness was over. They were in the Promised Land at last. Everything would be different now. Nothing would ever be the same again.

"It's When I Have to Wait that I Get Squeamish"

"I don't have time to be afraid when I'm in action. It's when I have to wait around and I don't know what's going to happen next that I get squeamish again. I really perform better when I'm in action. I'm not a very good wait-er."

Joshua may have felt the same way. For it was during these days that he went off by himself to size up Jericho. He didn't have a floor to pace, so he was probably pacing the grainfields. Jericho had to be taken. But how? And what now?

And then suddenly—

He looked up and saw a man right in the path in front of him. With a drawn sword in his hand!

Now Joshua could have turned and run. But he didn't. He walked up to the man. "Are you for us, or for our enemies?" he said. Which meant: "What ho? Who goes there? Are you friend or foe?"

And talk about surprises!

The stranger said something that made Joshua fall right on his face. "I am the Commander-in-Chief of the Lord's army." It was a few seconds before Joshua could even find his voice. And then—"Give me Your commands," he said, "what do You want me to do?"

The very first command was enough to make your head spin. "Take off your sandals," the stranger said, "for the place where you're standing is holy."

And Joshua did.

And the stranger* gave Joshua His battle plan, the instructions for taking Jericho.

But?!?

But meanwhile, what of the people inside Jericho? What was going on there? What *had* been going on? Had they known about the spies that Joshua had sent? What were they doing? How did they feel?

You'll find out all about it in the next two chapters. And about the spies' adventures inside the city. And about a woman who lived there—and who got into this story unexpectedly one night when she heard a knock on her door . . .

Meanwhile, What About You?

Moses was a hard leader to follow. And Joshua must have had his moments of squeamishness. But if Joshua did any worrying, he did it all for nothing.

For the God of Moses was with him. And the Bible tells us that "the Lord made him great in the eyes of all the people of Israel, and they revered him as much as they had Moses, and respected him deeply all the rest of his life."

The God who was with Moses and Joshua is the same God who will be with you. "He is the same—yesterday, today, and forever."**

He has a personal interest in you, and in everything you do. And He has a plan for you, the same as He had a plan for Joshua. If you put your life in His hands, and let *Him* do your planning, He says, "I will be with you . . . I will not abandon you or fail to help you."***

*Who was the Lord!
**Hebrews 13:8
***Joshua 1:5 (TLB)

64

7

You Never Know When You're Going to Meet God

Joshua 2

It was a beautiful city, there in the Jordan valley. It stood out like a jewel in the midst of the dry plains around it, and the palm trees and balsam flourished* there, for the springs of fresh water were plentiful.

Jericho!

People nicknamed it "The City of Palm Trees."

It was very, very rich. And very, very wicked.

And it was heavily fortified.

Strong double walls surrounded it, with houses built right into them. The huge gates were guarded by day—and locked and guarded by night.

Which wasn't a bad idea, for Jericho was an important city, a strategic city—indeed it was the gateway to the west.

Anyone who wanted to conquer the land of Canaan would have to conquer Jericho first . . .

*They grew like crazy!

What? You Haven't Found Him? He Knows Where You Are

The two strangers walked along the busy winding streets, mingling with the crowds, jostled and being jostled—and listening.

Here they stopped at the edge of a crowd to watch a fight between two peasant boys. There they rested in the shade of a narrow alleyway, pretending to snooze, catching snatches of conversation as people hustled by.

They dawdled* in the "Broad Place," just inside the gate, where people came to settle their business affairs and to gossip. And they listened. And listened.

The gossip was all about the one thing that was on everyone's mind. The great and terrible multitude of people just across the Jordan River.

The Israelites—led by Joshua!

It was useless to fight them. They had a living God who performed miracles. The old-timers told how He had parted the waters of the Red Sea and the Israelites had walked across it on dry land! Forty odd years ago, it was. Many of them remembered hearing about it firsthand, when it happened.

And now, this army of Joshua's was on its way toward Jericho—almost sure to attack it. All they had to do was get across the Jordan River.

Everyone was scared to death.

The two strangers slumped, snoozed—and listened.

They were the two spies Joshua had sent.

When they'd heard enough, they got up—and moved on lazily—down the street—up an alley—toward the city wall.

It was getting along toward sundown.

You Never Know When He'll Knock on Your Door

Now in that city lived a woman, who may have lived her

---

*They "hung around."

68

life and died and never been heard of again, except that God had singled her out to weave her into the pattern of His plans. She was an innkeeper.

Her name was Rahab.

And the house in the wall that these two spies came to was hers.

"Just a minute!" she cried from inside the house, at their insistent knocking. She hurried to the door, unbolted it, and squeaked it open.

"May we lodge here?" the two spies said.

"Who are you?"

"We only ask shelter for the night. Does it matter who we are?"

"Come in," she said. But she had hesitated.

"You seem frightened," they said.

"Who isn't frightened?" she shot back. "Everybody's scared to death. With an army ready to march on us—" And then she stopped, as if she'd suddenly got them into focus.* "You're not from Jericho. You're not one of us. You—you're Israelites."

No answer.

"Aren't you?" she persisted.

"Will you let us stay?"

"If you're found here, I'll be killed."

"We won't be found," they said. "Our God is watching over us. He has given us this city."

"Your God," she said. "The Living God of Israel. God in heaven above—God of all the earth. I know." She had backed up, and they had stepped inside the house.

The Things You've Heard About Him Are True

They stared at each other in the gloom.

"You seem to know us very well," they said.

*Saw them clearly.

"Is it true that He parted the waters of the Red Sea for His people?" She was bolting the door behind them.

"It is true."

"Some don't believe it. I believe it. I—I believe that He's given you this city too. He must be a wonderful God."

"Do we stay?"

"You stay. I'll risk it. Out this way. You may wash. I'll get you something to eat."

Rahab was risking more than she knew. For someone in the town had seen the two spies, the proper authorities had been notified—and already the news had reached the king!

If You Believe It You Have to Act on It

It was late evening now. The city was restless and uneasy. There was fear in the very air, as people began to disappear from the streets, and lights in the windows began to go on.

Rahab had gone to prepare a room for the strangers. She was leaning out the window to close the shutters when she saw something that froze her to a standstill.

It was a squadron of soldiers* coming down the street. And they were headed in the direction of her house! She whirled around, back to the room where the strangers were waiting.

"Soldiers," she said, "coming this way. They'll be banging on the street door in a minute."

"Can you hide us?"

"There's no place. They may search the house. Except the roof! There's the roof! Come on—quickly!"

They scuffled up the stairs, stumbling over each other, to the roof. Rahab crouched, scooted over to where huge stalks of flax** were spread out on the roof to dry, began to scrape them together.

*You might call them MP's today.
**People spread stalks of flax on their roofs to dry in the sun.

70

"Come over here—lie down—over here—*keep low!* You can be seen from the street. Here. I'll cover you up with flax stalks."

She did, working feverishly. Then, crouching, she crossed the roof to the stairs, and, brushing the flax fibers from her clothing, went back down, her knees wobbling all the way. Inside the house again, she bent over a candle, lighted it, her hand shaking. The light shot her shadow up the side of the wall like a giant, when—

There it was. The loud knocking, the voices outside.

She unbolted the door, opened it, stared out into the twilight.

It was the soldiers.

"Yes?" She squinted out at them.

"We are looking for Israelite spies. They were seen coming this way."

She stared at them, blinking, stalling for time.

"They were seen coming in here," they said. "Let us in—in the name of the king."

The jig was up.

"Oh—THOSE men," Rahab was thinking fast.

"Then you have seen them?"

"Yes—they came here. Who were they?" As if she hadn't heard.

"Spies. From Joshua's army."

"Spies! Well, two strangers did come here but they've gone. They went toward the city gates. I'll wager they got out just before the gates were closed for the night."

"Did they say where they were going?"

"No—but if you go quickly, you can overtake them. They can't have gone far!"

They stared at her for an instant. They decided to believe her. The next moment they were gone.

Phew!

She closed the door, leaned against it, trembling. After a minute she bolted the door, picked up the candle and car-

71

ried it to her room. She forced herself to move slowly. Her knees were like Jello. She set the candle down on a stand, blew it out—

—then dashed for the stairs to the roof! She crouched, scooted over to the piles of flax.

"They've gone!" she hissed.

If You Want to Belong to Him, You Have to Ask

The two spies crawled out, followed Rahab down from the roof. They went to a window that looked out from the city wall, and peered into the darkness. Even though they knew the soldiers had gone, they still whispered.

"I know perfectly well that your God is going to give you this land," she told them. "We are all afraid of you." She crossed the room, rummaged through a cupboard. "We tremble and quake when the word *Israel* is even mentioned." And she came back to the window carrying a length of heavy cord. It was red. "We know that you've mowed down everything in your path on your way here." And she anchored the cord to the window sill, zig-zagging it around the shutter-hinges, the hardware, anything she could get her hands on. They began to help. "No one has any fight left in him after hearing tales like that. There is fear in the very air!"

Ah! They were finished. The rope was secure.

"I'll let you down the outside wall. You can hide in the mountains until they've given up the search for you. But first—"

She dropped the end of the cord out into the darkness and turned to face them.

"I pray you—since I've shown you this kindness—that you will show me and my family kindness—"

"What would you have us do?"

"Spare our lives—my mother and father—my sisters and

brothers, and their families—when you come back to take the city."

"You ask a great deal."

"I know. Will you promise?"

"We will promise. If you promise not to tell anyone of our mission here. *Anyone.*"

"No, no, I won't tell anyone."

"When we come back—leave a portion of this red cord hanging from your window. And get your family all into this house. *Only those found in this house will be saved.*"

"All right."

"If they—or you—go out from this house when the attack begins, or if you betray us to anyone, your blood will be on your own head. We won't have to keep the promise."

"Yes, yes. It will be as you say."

She held her breath as they let themselves out the window, hand over hand, down the rope. Then they disappeared, silent, into the darkness.

No one had seen them.

You Don't Feel Saved? Wait and See!

The days that followed were busy ones for Rahab. She had to get to her father and mother and brothers and sisters and their families. She had to get *through* to them—to convince them that her house was the only safe place to be if Jericho was attacked.

The gates of the city were kept closed all the time now. And the fear grew and grew.

Rahab watched over the plains from the upper window. She strained her eyes toward the River Jordan.*

And she made sure the red cord was still there. She anchored it and reanchored it, a hundred times.

How would they get across the Jordan River?

*Which was about five miles away.

That was the question in Jericho.

The Jordan River was deep and wide. And right now it was overflowing its banks. They might send a few men across—but how could they send a whole army?

The Military Intelligence force of Jericho was working overtime—watching every move the Israelites made.

You Ask God into Your Life—He'll Come

On the day it happened, the soldiers on reconnaissance duty were probably out scouting. And their eyes must have bulged when they saw the front ranks of that great army marching right down to the river banks.

"What do you suppose they're going to do?"

"They seem to be just waiting."

"What is the box they carry by poles on their shoulders?"

"It's the Ark—I've heard it's the most sacred place of the Spirit of their living God. It always goes with them. They—"

"Wait! They're stepping—toward the water—No! The fools!"

"They're walking—right into the river!"

"No! *They're walking—on a dry path THROUGH the river.*"

"The water on the north has stopped flowing down!"

"The water on the south has gone on down to the sea—the river bed here is dry!"

"They're walking across the river!?!!"

"Run! Run tell the king! RUN FOR YOUR LIVES!"

Yes.

There was unbelievable adventure ahead.

Think a Minute

Well, Rahab took a whopping big step in faith. She didn't say, "I believe in God, all right, but I'm afraid to do anything about it. We have a king here in Jericho who's a terror. He's wicked, *very* wicked. If I let you stay here, my life wouldn't be worth a shekel.*

Or she could have turned the spies in, when the soldiers came a-rapping.

But she did neither.

She believed God *all the way*, and cast her lot** with His people. And when the soldiers came to drag the spies out as criminals, she protected them, for she knew they were not.

Does God Use Only Very Special People?

"Rahab was pretty special, after all, with all that derring-do. She must have been an important person to dare to stand up to the soldiers—and a wicked king."

Wrong.

Rahab was an innkeeper, and women who were innkeepers in those days did not have very good reputations. Actually, Rahab was a nobody; in a test for earth-shaking ability, she would have come out about minus one on the Richter Scale.

So stand up tall and shake the dust off; there's a lot for you to do. The important thing about Rahab's faith was that *she did something about it*.

And while you're shaking the dust off, read James 2:25. And Hebrews 11:31.

You see, they were still raving about her hundreds of years later!

*About a dollar.
**She chose to join them, come what may!

75

8
The Safest Place to Be

Joshua 5 and 6

The people of Jericho knew the worst, even before the scouts came back. The guards had seen it from the watchtowers at the city gate, their eyes straining toward the Jordan River, their hearts failing them for fear.

The swollen waters of the flooding Jodan had been between them and the great army of Israelites.

And now, incredibly, the Israelites had gotten across.

When the gates of Jericho were opened to the scouts, they fell, half dead with fright.

"They're coming!"

"They stop for nothing!"

"They walk across rivers!"

"We are doomed!"

Rahab heard it, there in the Broad Place by the gate. She hurried home, went up to that certain window, felt the red cord, made sure it was still there, anchored, safe, hanging down the outside wall. That cord meant everything. That cord meant salvation for her—and for her family.

Her heart beat fast. She shaded her eyes, peered across the plain toward the Jordan. They'd be coming now, any day, any hour. The Israelites—and God.

77

HER God now, too.

It's Confusing? Just Wait; It'll Clear Up

What happened?

As far as the Military Intelligence in Jericho could see—nothing. At least nothing of military significance. There were no battering rams, no chariots—and no watchtowers* were being built. None of the operations you'd expect to be going on, were going on.

Not one.

The Israelites just seemed to be resting. And eating.**

Meanwhile the orders were flying thick and fast inside Jericho. The gates were to be closed now at all times, not just at night. No one was to come in without being questioned and searched. No one was to go out without permission from the king.

A state of emergency was declared.

Everyone was terrified—but Rahab. She was a little frightened—yet with a strange new hope that made her eager for the great army to come. When she went to get water, she hurried back to her house, dashed to that upper window to see if anything had happened while she was gone. If any of the others wanted to go out—her mother or father or sisters or brothers—they had to answer to her first. She was so afraid they'd be gone too long, or perhaps wouldn't come back at all.

It was hard to make them believe that they HAD to be in her home when the attack took place. They had to take her word for it, in blind faith.

Every morning she'd awaken thinking, "Today's the day."

*Besieging armies often built rough "towers" outside the city wall, high enough to peek into the city.

**They were celebrating the Feast of the Passover.

And she'd rush to the window and look across the plains.

Nothing. Absolutely nothing.

God Does Some Things in the Strangest Ways

And then one morning she saw them.

Way across the plain, she saw them. Clouds of dust, specks in the distance—they were coming!

Others had been watching, too, and before she got downstairs to tell the family, the cry was going up all over the city! Everywhere people crowded to see—people in windows, people on rooftops—watching, hardly daring to breathe.

And then, as they drew closer, people scampered down from rooftops—some to hide in the center of town, some to stay by their possessions and save them if they could. The armed men were stationed by the walls and gates.

And so they watched and waited.

Strange!

The Israelite army!

The warriors came first, armed with swords and shields and bows and arrows and slings and spears.

And then—holy men all dressed in white—seven of them —and they carried strange trumpets made from rams' horns!

Behind them were more men in white robes with something—something that glittered in the sun like gold. It WAS gold. It was the sacred Ark of God, that strange and beautiful box they carried by poles on their shoulders. It had two carved figures on top with outspread wings, and it was gold, all of it.

It was dazzling in the sun.*

*Actually they covered it with a blue cloth when they carried it. Just thought **you'd** like to know what was underneath!

And then, as far as they could see, more warriors. There seemed to be no end to them.

It was so quiet.

There was no shouting, no battle cry, no military orders, no call for a parley. No one spoke at all. There was absolute silence.

And then—

The men with the rams' horn trumpets lifted them to their lips and began to blow!

They were eerie, bone-chilling blasts that bounced against the walls and froze the people's hearts with terror, and echoed and re-echoed over the plains of Jordan.

The first in the procession started around the city walls, and the rest followed. All the way around the city. And then —when the first ones got back to where they'd started, they marched away in the direction from which they'd come! And the others followed. Without a word, without even an upward look—they came—and went.

Stranger!

It was a trick. It was a TRICK. A war of nerves, that's what it was. They'd be back that night for a surprise attack. The guards were doubled. A watch was kept. No one dared sleep. All through the long night, they waited.

Nothing happened.

The next morning, sure enough, they could be seen in the distance—all of them. The Ark could be seen, and the men in white robes. They were coming again. This time to fight!

But no. Without a word, they marched around the city again and without a word they were gone as they had before, the trumpet blasts fading away in the distance, and leaving an eerie silence.

For six days they did that, marched around once, and were gone. For six nights, all Jericho waited for some trick, some surprise attack, that never came. They were exhausted; the tension was almost unbearable. They watched, from the top of the gate, from the outer wall, from all the windows of all the houses along the top of the wall—

And then it was the seventh day.

Stranger Yet

Rahab and her family were watching too. Sure enough, the Israelites came back—the priests with white robes, the golden box, the trumpets too. They began that march around the walls *again*. Rahab watched from her window until the first ones got to the starting point again, then started to turn away—

But wait!

The warriors who headed the procession weren't starting back to the Israelite camp this time. They were starting around the city walls again!

She called to her father to keep watch. She was downstairs to the street door in a flash, making sure everybody was in the house. Then there was the flurry of closing windows, bolting doors, counting noses. And checking in with her father all the while.

"What are they doing, father?"

"They've started around yet another time. This is the third time."

"Third time?!? This is the day, then. Something's going to happen. Is the cord in plain sight from the window?"

"Yes, yes. It's here."

"Is it secure?"

"It's secure."

"Then everything's all right. We'll just wait—and see."

Strangest!

It was hours later. No one had even thought of food.

They were unutterably weary.*

It's a foolish thing to do, Rahab," her father said.

"What, just waiting?"

"No—this marching around and around. What can they hope to accomplish? They are not setting up for a siege. These walls are double. And thick. And high."

"I know," she said, "but their God doesn't work in ordinary ways. He—" She stopped short. "How many times have they gone around now?"

"It's been six—no, seven. They've started around the seventh time I think."

"Perhaps—perhaps the whole city will yet surrender. They've had ample time to surrender, haven't they, Father?"

"They will never surrender. They—Rahab, listen."

Now the trumpets were blowing. One long, loud ear-splitting blast.

"Something will happen now," Rahab said. "Those trumpet blasts are longer. They're not stopping. They're—"

The rest of what she said was swallowed up in noise!

You Believe What You See**

After the last long, loud blast of the trumpets, Joshua yelled to the people, "Shout! SHOUT! FOR THE LORD HAS GIVEN US THE CITY!"

And the great cry that went up from the multitude outside the city walls was terrible to hear! "Jehovah has given us this city! Jericho is ours in the name of Jehovah!"

The roar was like thunder! It was more than shouting, louder than—

Wait a minute.

It was the walls!

---

*That's so tired you can hardly stand up.

**Rahab believed what she saw before her eyes. You believe what you see in God's Word.

THE WALLS!!!

The very earth seemed to rent and give way beneath them! Big jagged cracks zig-zagged their way up the outer walls, and they came crashing outward—dragging the inner walls along with them. And the houses that were built upon them all came down, down, ripping, crashing, tearing, sprawling down the hillside! Homes were turned inside out as if by some giant hand, their contents spilling all askew.*

People leapt from windows, fought their way farther into the city, climbed blindly over rubble through the confusion and the dust and the fire—

Fire!

It was springing up everywhere, choking, blinding—

FIRE!

And the orders went forth, and the Israelite army poured into the city, from every side, every man "straight before him." And Joshua shouted to the two spies—

"Keep your promise."

Old Things Are Passed Away**

A little group of soldiers led by the two spies started off, in the direction of the portion of the wall where Rahab's house would be. And there it was, beginning to sag—ugly jagged cracks finding their way up toward it, the walls on both sides of it bending outward crazily, fire eating its way all around it. And there it was—

The scarlet cord in the window!

Heads in the window, too. Rahab and her father had seen the soldiers.

The heads in the window disappeared when the soldiers got close. The cracks in the wall widened. The two spies hur-

---

*All jumbled up. Like your room when you don't clean it.

**When someone becomes a Christian he becomes a brand new person inside. He is not the same any more. A new life has begun! 2 Corinthians 5:17 (TLB)

ried around to the other side, the soldiers following, into the choking, blinding dust and smoke. And at last they pounded on Rahab's door. It opened immediately.

Rahab was framed in the doorway, her hair streaming down, her eyes swollen from the stinging smoke. And her family, their faces masks of terror, all with their bundles of precious possessions, only what they could carry.

There was no time for words. The soldiers grabbed bundles, and half dragged that frightened family over the debris—keeping a safe distance from that sagging wall.

When they were outside, they turned to watch, their faces sagging with shock. The last section of the wall bent, lurched crazily, and then with a tremendous groan, plunged outward, dragging Rahab's house and the inner wall with it!

All Things Are Become New!

The last thing Rahab saw before it crumpled into nothingness, was the window with the scarlet cord dangling from it.

And as they stood and watched, the city was destroyed utterly—by fire and by the sword. Every possession was destroyed, except the silver and gold utensils of bronze and iron that went into the Lord's treasury.

Rahab was saved. She had *just believed God*.

You're Saved for a Purpose!

She was not only saved from destruction—she was saved for a glorious destiny.* As she stood there, clutching her robes about her, hugging her bundle of possessions, pushing her streaming hair from her face—she could see only smoke and flames and a crumpled city wall. Where she could NOT

*A life God had already planned for her!

see—was down through the years, when her name would be written in the most significant family tree of all times.

Rahab—
Mother of Boaz—
Who married Ruth—
Mother of Obed—
Whose son was Jesse—
Whose son was *David the king*.

And on through the years—from David to Joseph, husband of Mary—of whom was born, by God's Holy Spirit—

Jesus!

How could she know as she stood there, the glorious destiny that was hers? She only knew she was saved—by faith.

She wiped her face on her sleeve, turned wearily away—and, with her family, followed the soldiers who had charge of her, to safety.

Stop and Think

Rahab cast her lot with God, with nothing to go on. You have the Word of God to go on. And He says, "Believe on the Lord and thou shalt be saved . . ." And "Whosoever believeth on Him should not perish but have everlasting life."

She had no idea what God's plans were for the future. You have one up on her there, for you *do* know. He has told us that He is coming again (John 14:1-3).

But What About Today?

"What about me, now, today?"

Well, when all this happened, it was "today" for Rahab. The safest place to be that day was in the city wall. The safest place for you today is in God's hands. *Now* is the day of salvation.

Rahab just put her faith in God and trusted Him to "take it from there." Here's Psalm 37:5:

"Commit everything you do to the Lord.
Trust Him to help you do it—
And He will." (TLB)

But first you must trust Him for your salvation. The Bible says, "Believe on the Lord and thou shalt be saved . . ." (Acts 16:31).

He's asking you to cast your lot with Him. It's the best offer you'll ever have in all your life. Nothing, but nothing, can match it!

9
What Have I Done Now and How Did You Find Out About It?

Joshua 7 and 8

If you have done something wrong and your conscience is nibbling at you, this is what you are apt to think whenever anybody looks at you strangely.

And you're apt to get so touchy that if anyone says "hello"—

You think, "What did he mean by that?"

This is especially true if you "borrow" something that doesn't belong to you. It is more accurately known as "stealing" and it means double-trouble. For once you've stolen something, you're stuck with it, and you have to hide it, or explain it. Or in one way or another, it becomes a pesky burden. It really isn't worth the bother, and anyone who is thinking two laps ahead wouldn't do it in the first place.

There are variations of course, but the run-down is usually something like this:

I saw it.

I wanted it.

I took it.

I hid it.

I'm stuck with it.

And then of course, there's always the reasoning behind the whole business: "It's not affecting anybody but me."

You Think So?

It's not affecting anybody but you?

There are many people who would give you an argument on this point.

Achan would be one if them, if he were here.

Who is Achan?

Well, Achan was an Israelite—one of the Israelites in Joshua's enormous army, in fact. Those were the days when God was first forming the great nation of Israel. The rules of the game were plain, and no one was allowed to break them; the punishment was swift and sure. God was training his new nation to set an example for ages to come, and He could afford no nonsense.

Jericho had just fallen.

And the Israelites were cleaning up the mess and getting out the loot.*

Remember the Loot-Rules?

Absolutely nothing was to be taken, no matter how valuable it might look. It belonged to the wicked Canaanites, and God did not want His people to have any part of it. The gold and silver and brass and iron were to be put aside for the treasury of the Lord.

There were certain men assigned to go in and take care of this business.

Achan was one of those men.

---

*It was called "spoils" in those days. It was all the things taken by the victor in war.

I Saw It

"Well, I saw this thing, you know. It was just something I always wanted. But I knew I could never have it. One of my dad's favorite remarks is, 'We can't afford it.' And he doesn't increase my allowance or allow for inflation or anything. Anyhow I didn't see any harm in just picking it up and turning it over to see how it looked and how it worked."

That's exactly what happened to Achan.

Jericho was in ruins. Some if it was still smoking. The Israelites were going methodically about the business of stripping it.

Achan was poking around a building. Had to stoop to get under a big beam that had fallen. Straightened up. Pushed his hair off his face. And blew his nose. Phew, that dust was awful. And it was hot, hot. And what they were doing was hard work. Everything had to be destroyed that *could* be destroyed. Everything that could *not* be destroyed, like metals—gold and silver and bronze and brass—had to be rooted out and set aside for the treasury of the Lord. There were jewels and gold nets for the hair and crescents for camels. There were candlesticks and jeweled perfume and ointment boxes and hair-ribbons made of fine beaten gold. There were carved chests filled with treasures and bronze and gold chests filled with finery—

Achan went kicking through the rubbish heap that had once been a wealthy home. Most of it had burned down. Most of it, but not all of it. He could hear the other soldiers calling back and forth to each other at their work—in the streets outside and in other buildings—

Hmmm. What was this?

A chest filled with treasures. Clothing, books, whatnots—

Ahhh. A robe. The most beautiful he'd ever seen. Must have been imported from Babylon. Brilliant colors, woven in intricate patterns. And the embroidery on it! Beautiful. Fit for a king.

He looked around to see if he was still alone.

91

It was lovely. Wouldn't hurt to just—hup—throw it over his shoulders.

Mmmmmm.

The luxury, just to feel of it. Just imagine wearing something like that. Why, he looked like royalty.

What else was in the box?

A wedge of gold. Must weigh 50 shekels* if it weighed one. And here—silver. A few pieces? No, a lot of it. Two hundred shekels,** at least.

I Wanted It

"I thought about how nice it would be to have it. And then I thought about how nobody would miss it anyway. And I even thought about how if I didn't take it, maybe it would just go to waste. Maybe nobody would get any good out of it at all. *I'd* sure get some good out of it. And nobody need ever know—" Well, Achan might have had a conversation with himself at this point:

"You are alone, Achan—"

"No—no—"

"Still—it would be nice to have—if you had that money and that valuable robe. You've never had anything like that before—"

"I know—"

"You've always worn homespun homemade clothes. If you had that—and saved it—someday you'd be a wealthy man, when you got settled down—"

"Yeah. It's such a little bit to them. They have the whole city full of riches to put in the Lord's treasury. They'll never miss it."

"You're right. It's such a little bit."

"Yes—compared with the wealth in this whole city. It couldn't be too wrong. After all, I'm not robbing my brother

*$50.

**$200.

92

or my neighbor—just taking a small helping of a big pile that belonged to my enemies. Oh, oh. What if I'm caught?"

"You can hide it. You could dig a hole in the bottom of your tent and hide it."

"But I can't hide it alone. My family would have to know."

"They'll understand. It's such a little bit. No one else will know. It's your own personal business."

"Yes. It's my own personal business."

I Took It

"Well, the chances were good that I'd get away with it. Nobody was stopping me. I mean, nobody even *knew*. Anyhow, I didn't have to argue with myself about it any longer."

"I just took it."

So it was with Achan.

There was that moment when he had to make a choice, to make up his mind.

"Hooooooooooo." Voices from outside. "Anything in there?"

And Achan made his choice. "No—not a thing. I—I'm coming right out!" And he stuffed the loot back into the chest, pushed it farther into a corner, covered it with rubbish—and climbed through the ruins and back out into the street. His heart was beating so hard, it hurt.

All the rest of the day he helped the others tug at the treasures and carry them off. All afternoon he said very little. His mind was on what he had done. His mind was on what he must do. He had to get the loot back to his tent without being discovered.

I Hid It

"Well, after I got it home, I didn't know what to do with

it. I didn't dare show it to anybody. Everybody would know right off that I didn't buy it. So I hid it. What else could I do? I hid it, and now I hope nobody finds out what I've done."

Achan had the same problem. The Bible doesn't tell us exactly how he managed it, but somehow he got the beautiful robe and the wedge of gold and two hundred shekels of silver back to his tent.

And then there was the sneaky digging, inside the family tent, and the loot was buried, first the silver, then the rest on top of it.

What else could he do? He hid it, and hoped nobody would find out what he had done.

I'm Stuck with It

You're stuck with your choices, all right. That's why it's a pretty good idea to be careful what choices you make. Achan buried his loot, but that wasn't the end of it. At first it might have seemed like it. As the days went by, the business of living pushed the memory of his sin into the background. And then—

Orders to attack Ai!

Ai was the next city to conquer.

The spies who had been sent ahead, came back with good news. "Easy," they said. "Nothing to it. We can wipe them out with only a few men. Say, two—three thousand at the most." So about three thousand men went up to Ai on what they thought was a routine mission. But they'd hardly got within shouting distance when—

The armies of Ai swarmed out of the city gates like a thunder clap and chased Joshua's men down the hill and clear to the quarries. And while they were stumbling through the rocks, thirty six of them were killed. Not Ai men. *Joshua's* men.

What a stunning blow!

And what was wrong?
Plenty.
There was trouble ahead.

It's Not Affecting Anyone but Me

"*I* did it. And if I *do* get caught, I'm the only one who'll
have to suffer. So it's none of anybody else's affair."

That's what *you* think. And that's what Achan thought.
But Achan was dreaming while he was walking around.

The debacle* at Ai could mean only one thing.

God had not been with them. They'd bungled into this
defeat for some reason. What was wrong?

Joshua and his elders got down before the Lord. "What
shall we do?" And, "When the other Canaanites hear about
this, they'll wipe us out!" And, "What will happen to the
honor of Your great name?" And, "What's *wrong?!!?*"

And God said to Joshua, "Get up." And then God told
Joshua in no uncertain terms, exactly what was wrong. Israel
had sinned. Israel had taken loot that was forbidden and
loot that belonged to God. Israel had lied and hidden it.
Israel had—

What's this? Israel? *Israel?*

Yes, Israel.

"That is why your men are running from their enemies,"
said God. "Someone has stolen from Me. And I cannot be
with you until you rid yourselves of this sin."

Achan's sin was not affecting anyone but Achan?
Not so.
Achan's sin was affecting all of Israel!

The Deed Is Done; What Next?

The answer is simple.

*The sudden smashing collapse!

95

Confess it!

Confession is absolutely the shortest way back to the right road. Any other way will lead you into pits, holes, dead-end streets, detours, tunnels and traps. Any other way is the long way around.

Achan knew.

He took the other way.

The next morning, the most amazing probe* in history took place. The entire camp of Israel—thousands upon thousands of them—were summoned and told to march past Joshua and the elders. God had told Joshua He would point out the man who had sinned.

That was when Achan should have owned up. But he didn't. He waited, hoping he would not get found out. The Israelites marched past by tribes. On and on they came, past Joshua and the elders—

The tribes of Reuben—Simeon—Levi—

Achan kept quiet. He belonged to the tribe of Judah.

The tribes of Dan—Gad—Asher—

Achan had a chance to own up. But he kept quiet.

The tribes of Benjamin—Judah—

Judah! JUDAH WAS THE TRIBE!

Achan had another chance to own up. But he kept quiet.

God Is the God of Many Chances!

Then the tribe of Judah marched past by clans.**

Achan kept quiet. He belonged to the clan of Zerah.

On and on they came, past Joshua and the elders—

Clan after clan after clan—

Zerah! ZERAH WAS THE CLAN!

Achan had another chance to own up. But he kept quiet.

Then the clan of Zerah marched past by families.

*They snooped into the matter to find out what was wrong.
**Groups of families.

96

Achan kept quiet. He belonged to the family of Zabdi.

On and on they came, past Joshua and the elders—

Family after family after family—

Zabdi! ZABDI WAS THE FAMILY!

Achan had *another* chance to own up. But he kept quiet.

Then the family of Zabdi marched past, person by person.

Achan had ANOTHER chance to own up. But he kept quiet.

On and on they came, past Joshua and the elders—

Achan marched by, his eyes straight ahead. But the sweat was streaming down his face. On and in he marched, past Joshua and the elders—

Achan! ACHAN WAS THE MAN!

"Bring him to me," said Joshua. "He is the one."

Achan's last chance was gone.

But There IS an End!

Yes. God is a God of many chances. But there *is* an end to them, finally. And confessing voluntarily* is a far cry from admitting your guilt after you've been caught red-handed.

"My son," said Joshua, "tell me what you have done."

And Achan blurted it out. *Finally.* "I have sinned against the Lord, the God of Israel," he said, "For I saw a beautiful robe imported from Babylon, and some silver worth $200 and a bar of gold worth $50. I wanted them so much that I took them, and they are hidden in the ground beneath my tent, with the silver buried deeper than the rest."**

Joshua sent men for the loot. And they brought it back and spread it on the ground before him. "You have brought calamity*** upon us!" thundered Joshua.

*On your own!

**Joshua 7:20,21 (TLB)

***Trouble—BIG trouble.

Indeed it was true.

Achan's sin did not involve just him alone. His family was involved. Thirty-six soldiers had been killed. Many had been wounded. Achan had had chance after chance after chance to confess—

But he had *not* confessed, and now the jig was up.

The sentence was death. To Achan and his family.

God just took them all home a little early, before they got into any more mischief.

How About You?

If you are ever tempted by the "I saw it—I want it" routine —forget it.

It isn't worth it.

In one way or another, it becomes a pesky burden.

If you are going through this routine—remember, confession is absolutely the shortest way back to the right road. Any other way will lead you into pits, holes, dead-end streets, detours, tunnels and traps. Any other way is the long way around.

What? You're not being tempted? And you're not going through this routine?

Well, memorize 1 John 1:9 anyhow. It will cover any little sin you might be dabbling in. What? You're not dabbling? Then memorize verse 10 too. *That* will shut you up!

10

The Man
Who Stopped the Sun

Joshua 9 and 10

Ever hear of the League of Nations? Well, then, you've heard of the United Nations. Did you think they were something new?

Not so.

There was a league of nations more than 3,000 years ago. It concerns five wicked kings, the great nation of Israel, one of the biggest hoaxes* of history—and Joshua.

There's Something Sneaky Going on Around Here

A worried servant hurried along a corridor in the palace, stopped at the door of the king's quarters, and knocked.

No answer. The guards were asleep. And in the room beyond, the king was asleep. This fellow awakened them all, and then there was the flurry of baths, breakfast trays and royal robes—

It was going to be a busy day.

For the King's name was Adoni-zedek, and he was the

---

*A hoax is a practical joke, to fool someone—only this one wasn't funny.

chap who had organized this first league of nations. All the kings of the land of Canaan were involved.* They'd got together because they were afraid—afraid of Joshua and the Israelites, who were sweeping into the land of Canaan, conquering everything before them. They were said to have a living God—indeed no man could stand against them.

An hour later, in one of the downstairs rooms of the palace, around a highly polished conference table, sat all the big-wigs of the land of Canaan. The kings were there, and their right-hand men, and their generals. Adoni-zedek was speaking, and as he spoke, his finger traced an imaginary map on the table and everyone watched intently.

"I have in my possession," he said, "The details of the fall of Jericho—here." His finger stopped, moved on—"and the capture of Ai—right—here. According to the information at my disposal, the next city they will attack is the capital city of the Hivites—the city of Gibeon. Right—here." His finger stopped at an imaginary "Gibeon" on the table. Silence.

Then every eye turned to the rulers of Gibeon. And the rulers of Gibeon didn't feel so good.

The Big Set Up

The rulers of Gibeon were badly frightened; in fact they felt so bad they went home and called a council, and wore a path in their red plush carpets with their pacing. And they finally came up with a unanimous** conclusion.

"Peace!"

"We must make peace with these Israelites—somehow!"

And this is what they did.

They took four men and fixed them up as though they had been on a long journey. A loooooooong journey.

---

*Their names were a mouthful: The Hittites, the Amorites, the Canaanites, the Perizzites, the Jebusites and the Hivites.

**They all agreed, to the last man.

Matted hair.

Straggly beards.

Worn-out clothing.

Patched, worn-out shoes

Weatherworn saddlebags on their donkeys.

Old, patched wineskins.

Dry, mouldy crusts of bread.

It was a thorough job. And then they told these men what they must do . . .

The Big Hoax

A while later, the Israelites were surprised to see four men come limping into their camp, worn-out, in fact utterly *exhausted*.

"What ho?" they cried. "Who goes there?"

"We have come from a far away country,"* the fakers said, "and we've come to make a peace pact with you."

"Peace? Peace?" said the Israelites. "And how do we know you're not from one of the nearby cities? One of the very cities we plan to attack? For if you are, you know, we can't make any peace treaty with you."

"Gentlemen, GENtlemen," the fakers said, "we are CRUSHED. We came to be your servants. How can you doubt us?"

"But just who *are* you?" Joshua demanded. "Exactly where do you come from?"

"We are from a very distant country; we've heard of the might of the Lord your God, and of all the marvelous things He did in Egypt. And how you've been mowing everything down before you. So we were instructed to prepare for a long journey, and to come here and declare our nation to be your servants—and to ask for a peace treaty."

Joshua and his men still stared in unbelief.

*Why the rascals had come only a few miles!

"Gentlemen," the fakers hurried on, "look. Just look at our shoes, patched and ready to drop off. And look at these mouldy bread crusts. See? Why they were practically hot out of the oven when we started, and now—

"Taste them. Aren't they *awful?*

"And look at our wineskins!" they cried, warming to their subject. "Why they were brand new when we started. Oh, we've come a long way. A loooooooooong way."

And they stood there drooping, very convincingly.

So convincingly, in the fact, that Joshua and the other leaders believed them. And signed a peace treaty with them. And ratified the agreement with a binding oath!*

And all of this nonsense, on their own!

For the Bible tells us: *They did not bother to ask the Lord.*

They just went ahead and *did* it!

So you can see right off, that they're in for some trouble.

The Big Awakening

Well, the Israelites rested up these "exhausted" gentlemen, and then part of Joshua's army started on the march to Gibeon. It was only a few miles, and when they got there, the awful news came out.

And the old fakers confirmed it.**

"Hi, neighbors," they said, in effect. "You can't TOUCH that city. It's ours. You just made a peace pact with it!"

Good grief.

The Big Blunder

It was true. The Israelites couldn't touch Gibeon. They'd sworn by God.

---

*It was one of those "cross-my-heart-and-hope-to-die" deals.
**Admitted that it was so.

104

It was the biggest hoax of the century!

The Israelites were licked, and they knew it.

"You—you Hivites of Gibeon!" the Israelite leaders stormed. "You've tricked us!"

And Joshua said, "For that, you will be wood-choppers and water-carriers for the people of Israel! You will be our servants forever!"

Well, that was all right with the Hivites of Gibeon. It was better to be living servants than dead enemies.

But Joshua had made peace with some of the very people God had ordered him to wipe out.

The Big Attack

But what of the other kings of the land of Canaan? They were alarmed. Especially Adoni-zedek. "Destroy Gibeon!" he bellowed. "Destroy them before they join forces with the Israelites and destroy *us!*"

And so the trumpets sounded, and all the armies of Canaan gathered to march against Gibeon.

The Hittites,

The Amorites,

The Canaanites,

The Perizzites,

And the Jebustites.

When the Hivites of Gibeon heard about it, they were in an uproar. They sent messengers to Joshua. "Come help your servants!" they demanded. "Come quickly and save us!"

So Joshua and his army left their camp at Gilgal and went to the rescue!

The Big Rescue

Joshua and his army made a forced march, through the night, up steep winding mountain country, loaded down

105

with bows and arrows and spears and armors and all the accoutrements* of warfare.

The five kings of Canaan were marching too, and their great armies camped around Gibeon. But all through the night, Joshua's army kept coming, coming, coming . . .

At dawn, when Adoni-zedek gave his order to "ATTACK!" He knew what was ahead of him—Gibeon!

(But he didn't know who had sneaked up behind him—JOSHUA! And the Israelites!)

It was one of the greatest battles in all history. They fought all morning, and in that part of the country at that time of year it was 120 in the shade. The sun was beating down on them without mercy. And then—!

The enemy broke ranks, and ran!

Joshua, the sweat streaming down his face, his tongue thick with thirst, cried, "After them!"

That was a big order. His soldiers were stunned with heat and exhaustion. But they ran after them.

And then—

We Have a Big God!

What's this?

A black cloud came over the sun! And though it never rained in that country through that part of the year—it not only rained that day—it HAILED! God turned on a mighty air conditioner. The air was washed and cooled, if you please. Can you picture it? Joshua's exhausted soldiers must have sucked on those chunks of hail and rubbed their faces with them and even put them down their necks.

They chased their enemies down the plain of Beth-horan, through the narrow rocky mountain passes and over the plains—but the hail-stones that God sent, killed more Canaanites than the swords of Joshua's army did!

*Their equipment, what little they had!

106

The chase went on.

But the day wore on, too. Time was flying. And the job wasn't done yet.

The Big Day

It was then that Joshua prayed and asked God for what seemed like the impossible.

"Oh, Lord God of Israel, help me!," he thought. And then—

"Let the sun stand still!" he cried. "Let the sun stand still over Gibeon, and let the moon stand in its place over the valley of Aijalon!"

What? *What?* Was he asking for time to stop?

He was asking for time to stop.

And it did!

The day went on and on and *on*—until it was almost as long as two!

The five kings of Canaan hid in a cave.

"What'll we do with them?" Joshua's soldiers wanted to know.

"Roll a great stone over the cave entrance," cried Joshua. "They'll keep! Go chase your enemies. To the very last one!"

And they did.

And the sun and the moon didn't move until the Israeli army had finished the job.

After the great battle was over, the kings were brought out of the caves and killed. And Joshua said, "Don't ever be afraid or discouraged. Be strong and courageous, for the Lord is going to do this to all your enemies."

What a battle it was! What a day it was!

If there had been radios then, a late bulletin might have gone something like this:

"Talkage speaking. Early this morning, one of the most spectacular battles of this war took place, is still taking place. The allied armies of Canaan fell upon Gibeon but

107

were repulsed by a surprise attack by the army of Joshua, which without warning appeared from nowhere and attacked their rear and right flank. They were surprised into the defensive, and the Gibeon army attacked their head and left flank. Squeezed between the jaws of a huge pincer movement, they retreated on the plains of Beth-horan. The retreat turned into a rout this afternoon. This looks like the end of organized resistance. Anything from here on out will be purely mopping-up operations. . . ."

Yes, indeed.

Never was there a day like it, before or since, when the Lord fought for Israel. When one day was made nearly as long as two.

God Keeps Big Records!

That battle—and that day—left an indelible record.

It left a record in God's Word. It left a record in the mythology of most every country in the world.

A Polynesian fable explains that long day like this:

They had a god in Polynesia—his name was Maui. And one day the great god Kane served notice on Maui's mother that he and some other gods were coming to supper. She prepared in a great flurry of excitement, and as the day wore on, she saw that she was not going to be ready in time. So she appealed to her super-son, Maui. Nothing daunted Maui. He climbed to the highest mountain, made a lasso out of cocoanut fibers, lassoed the sun, and . . . whoops, puuuuulled it down—and broke off all its legs! By the time the poor sun sat on the mountain-top to grow a new set of legs, almost another day had passed, and Maui's mother had time to get ready.

To this day, the long slanting rays of sun in the late afternoon are known there as the snares of Maui . . .

And it left a record in the sky. The astronomers have been telling us for years that no matter how they calculate it—

forward or backward—there's a day missing from time.

And recently, in our modern day of astronauts and space ships, our computers have been telling us the same thing.

There's a day missing from time.

"Wait a minute—wait a minute. The Bible says Joshua's long day was only ALMOST as long as two? What happened to the rest of it? Surely such a wonderful God wouldn't leave part of day just—just *dangling!*"

Of course He wouldn't. And he didn't.

Hundreds of years later, God stopped time again, for a king named Hezekiah. He stopped it for forty minutes.

But that's another story.

God Can Overrule Big Goofs

"All this power turned on for Joshua? He made a peace treaty without asking God! He goofed!"

Joshua wasn't perfect. God is still recruiting from the human race, remember?

Joshua depended on his own judgment, and that time his own judgment was a bit fuzzy. He absolutely goofed, and there's no getting around it. But he lived to regret it. He never lived to wipe out Canaan 100 percent.

For he had backed himself into a corner where he had to compromise with the people of Gibeon.

What About You?

If God can stop the sun, He can turn your life upside down. He has all the secrets. He has all the answers. If you really want to begin to live—put your life in God's hands. Put your life in God's hands, *in God's way.*

Jesus said, "I am the way, the truth and the life. No one comes to the Father, except by me."

And you couldn't be in better hands.

He is the God of the impossible!

11

The Name of the Game Is "Choice"

Joshua 11:1-23; 13:1-7; 22—24

Is That Any Way to End a Life?

You bet it is!

The rest of Joshua's rule was one long succession of victories. If they had been in newspaper headlines, they might have gone something like this:

KINGS OF THE NORTH FORM CONFEDERACY AGAINST JOSHUA!

CONFEDERACY HEADED UP BY JABIN, KING OF HAZAR

JOSHUA SCORES SMASHING VICTORY OVER CONFEDERACY!

JOSHUA VICTORIOUS OVER 31 KINGS!

ISRAELITES CONTROL LAND OF CANAAN!

COUNTRY AT REST FROM WAR

JOSHUA CELEBRATES 100th BIRTHDAY

Oh, oh. And God said to Joshua, just what you've been thinking. "You've grown old, Joshua," God told him. "Time to wind up your affairs."

And Joshua did.

There was still much land to be possessed. He divided it among all the tribes. And by the time he finished winding up all his affairs, he was 110 years old. His long and marvelous reign was over.

"What? Was He the Perfect Man?"

"Did he always do everything right? Didn't he ever make mistakes?"

Yes, of course he made mistakes. Nobody's perfect. And God was still recruiting from the human race, remember?

One of his greatest mistakes lived on with him to the end of his days. And long after he was gone. It was his mistake in believing those old rascals from Gibeon. He had done this without asking the Lord about it first, and he had trapped himself into a peace treaty with them. So the Israelites could never wipe them out!

You Have to Make a Choice

As a matter of fact, the entire land was sprinkled with heathen idol worshipers. So it didn't matter where the Israelites were. Somebody had a friend who had a friend who had a friend who was an idol worshiper. It was impossible to get away from them.

Now when you have nothing but good people surrounding you, it's pretty easy to be good. But if you have evil people sprinkled all around you and you have to rub elbows with them—then the name of the game is choice.

You can't get away from it. *You have to make a choice.*

This was the one big thing on Joshua's mind when he said his last farewell to his people.

First he called the leaders of the people together. He reminded them of what God had done. Not one good thing of all God's promises had failed. And then he warned them to stay close to God. "For it is the Lord your God who fights for you," he said, "as He promised you."*

And then he called all the people together at Shechem. From every direction they came pouring in—a great multitude of them. And with the two great mountains of Ebal and Gerazim towering above them, they gathered on the grassy slopes.

There they gathered, and there they heard Joshua speak to them for the last time. He reminded them of the wonderful way God had taken care of them. "You are here this day," he said, "safe in this land, living in homes you didn't build and eating food you didn't plant. And God has done all of this for you."

And then he put it to them straight.

"Which will it be?" he said. "Will you worship God?"

"Yes—Yes!" the people cried.

"Or will you worship idols?"

"No—never!" they cried. Perish the thought!

"You have to make up your minds," he said, "you can't have both."

And then he thundered the words that you probably cut your teeth on in Sunday School.

"Choose you this day whom you will serve!"

And then he showed that he was willing to stand up and be counted.

"As for me and my house—we will serve the Lord!"

"We choose the Lord too!" they cried back, "for He alone is our God!"

And then he nailed it down. "You have heard yourselves say it!" he cried. "You have chosen to obey the Lord!"

"Yes, *yes!*" they cried back. "We are witnesses!"

"All right, then," he said, "You must destroy all the idols you own. From here on out it is the Lord God of Israel. Alone."

*Joshua 23:10 **(Amplified)**

"Yes!" they cried back. "We will worship the Lord God alone."

But Joshua wasn't going to let them off the hook that easily. He had a huge stone rolled under the oak tree that was beside the Tabernacle. And he recorded what the people had said in the book of the Laws of God. Now it was in writing, a binding contract between the people—and God.

"It's all recorded!" he told them. "Everything you said. And this stone will be a witness!"

So there it was. All wrapped up. Legal and binding.

They had made a contract. And if they broke it, they had only themselves to blame. And they would suffer the consequences.

The name of the game was choice.

Forever Is a Long Time

That turned out to be one of the longest term contracts the world has ever known. For the rules of the contract have never changed. Down through the ages, every person who was ever born, ran into this contract sooner or later—and had to make a choice.

There was a young man, once, who had to make it. He had never thought much about God. The first time he ever went to church, he fell asleep. The first time he went to Sunday School, he was late. And he knew so little about his Bible that when the teacher told him the lesson was in the Gospel of John—he fumbled through the pages of the book of Genesis.

But he kept coming back, Sunday after Sunday. And every Sunday—no matter what the lesson was—the teacher brought up this business of choice. "You have to make a choice," he kept saying. "Jesus died for you. There is no other name under heaven by which you may be saved. Now is the day of salvation. Now is the day for you to make a choice."

Now all this boy had ever wanted to do, was grow up and make a lot of money. He'd never thought much about Jesus. But Sunday after Sunday, he kept hearing this word "choice"—like water dripping on his head.

Choice—
  choice—
    choice—
      choice—

He kept trying to put it out of his mind, but he couldn't. *Choice, choice, choice . . .*

And then one day, right smack in the middle of the week, while he was working in the back room of his uncle's shoe store—who should walk in to see him but his Sunday School teacher!

His Sunday School teacher? It wasn't even Sunday!

Well, it might not have been Sunday, but his teacher had been thinking about him all the same. And without pulling any punches, his teacher put his foot on a shoe carton, and his arm around this boy's shoulders. And he said, "Dwight," he said, "I've been telling you Sunday after Sunday about how much God loves you. And how Jesus died for you. And how He rose from the dead. And how He's coming again. He wants your love, Dwight. And He wants your life. And He deserves to have them both."

The two of them stood there for a moment in silence. Dwight thought about all his dreams of growing up and devoting his whole life to making a lot of money. And now he realized that he had to make a choice. He'd been putting it off long enough.

Choose you this day whom you will serve . . .

"Then I shall give Him my life," Dwight said at last.

He had made his choice.

He never went back on his word, either. The contract was binding, and he knew it. He had chosen that day whom he would serve. And it stayed with him for the rest of his life. He turned out to be one of the greatest evangelists the world has ever known. His name was Dwight L. Moody. And he was as well-known in his day as Billy Graham is today.

What About You?

You see you know too much, so you can't run off now. Once you've heard about Jesus, you have to make a choice. And there's no getting around it. You either have to choose Him and accept Him—or turn your back on Him.

Now he's not going to bind and gag you to make you accept Him. If He had to do that to get your love, then your love wouldn't be worth having.

He wants you to *choose* Him.

And that's what the whole business is all about.

Choose you *this day whom you will serve . . .

*This means **you.**

116

12

It's Too Much for Me

Judges 4 and 5

"Let Somebody Else Do It"

The modern way of saying it is "Leave me alone, I can't cope." No matter how you say it, anybody who has graduated from creeping to walking knows that this is the most convenient way to get things done. It works out very well, too, except when the law of averages catches up with you and the "somebody else" turns out to be you.

It's Nice Work If You Can Get Out of It.

Which is exactly what you sometimes want to do if it is at all possible and especially if you don't want to be a hero anyhow.

It was that way in Israel after Joshua died. For a time things worked out very well without his powerful leadership. And then Israel began to run down like a wooden clock. People had turned from God to the worship of idols. And things weren't going too well. Clearly, a hero was badly needed.

119

Now being a hero is all very well if you do so comfortably, like maybe just pressing buttons. But the truth of the matter was that being a hero in Israel in those days was pretty dangerous business. The Canaanites were invading Israel from the north. Jabin* was again in power, the commander of his army was Sisera, and the army was equipped with no less than nine hundred iron chariots. They had their stronghold at Hazor in northern Canaan and were making things so miserable for the Israelites that even travel on the public roads was dangerous. They stripped the Israelites of their weapons and the wretched Israelites had no chariots at all.

With a set-up like this, it would be a fine thing to be a hero—for somebody else.

A Heroine?!!?

Being a hero would be rough enough for a man—but a heroine is a *woman!*

Yes.

After the death of Joshua, Israel spent many years just stumbling and bumbling around—sometimes up, sometimes down.

And during this time, God raised up a whole succession of leaders to help the people out of their difficulties. They were military and spiritual leaders. And they were called judges. And one of these judges was a *woman.*

Her name was Deborah.

"But I'm Only a Girl. What Can I Do?"

"I'm not exactly cut out for derring-do. I'm not strong and I'm not brave. And in my wildest imagination I could never get out and lead an army. It's a case of 'I don't want it, you

*He's the king Joshua subdued . . . remember?

can have it, it's too much for me.' Let someone else do it!"

That's exactly the idea Deborah had in mind. She was not only a judge, you see—she was a prophetess.*

And God gave her, of all the people in Israel, a plan for defeating the Canaanites. She was to call upon an army general by the name of Barak, and give *him* the plan for marching against the Canaanites' most formidable** general. A chap by the name of Sisera.

"I'm With You All the Way—Almost"

Deborah sent for Barak. And the conversation might have gone something like this:

"Barak, the Lord God of Israel wants you to drive Sisera out of our country."

"Yes, Deborah. Good thinking."

"God has given me a plan, Barak."

"Let's hear the plan, Deborah."

"You are to call an army from your tribe of Naphtali and from your neighboring tribe Zebulun—"

"Yes, Deborah. The tribes nearest the stronghold of that rascal Jabin and his general Sisera and the Canaanites."

"Exactly, Barak. Get ten thousand men. And march them to Mount Tabor."

"Yes, Deborah."

"Sisera will find out that you are preparing to fight against him."

"Yes, Deborah."

"And when he finds out, he will come to battle with you. Near the River Kishon."

"Wait a minute, Deborah. How can I be sure he will meet me near the River Kishon. What if he decides to go someplace else?"

*God spoke to His people through her.
**Frightening, threatening, and just plain terrible.

121

"God will cause him to bring his army near the River Kishon, Barak. You can depend on it."

"Yes, Deborah."

"And God will give you victory over Sisera's army—"

"Yes, Deborah."

"Sisera's army of one hundred thousand men—"

"Yes, Deborah."

"And nine hundred chariots."

"Yes, Deb—Wait a minute."

"What is it, Barak?"

"*Nine hundred* chariots?"

"Yes, Barak."

"Heavier than Egyptian chariots?"

"Yes, Barak."

"Reinforced and strengthened with iron?"

"Yes, Barak."

"Deborah?"

"Yes, Barak?"

"I'll go. On one condition."

"Yes, Barak?"

"*If you go with me.*"

"I'll Go If You'll Go"

How many times have you heard *that* one? "I'll go to church if you'll go." "I'll carry my Bible if you'll carry *your* Bible." "I'll go on visitation and invite people to Sunday School if you'll go with me." "I'll sign up for camp if *you'll* sign up for camp." "I'll go to VBS if *you'll* go to VBS." The "I'll go if you go" routine is a very old cop-out. And a pretty flimsy one too.

"But You're Asking Too Much!"

"Visitation is pretty scary business. And carrying a Bible is too. I get embarrassed and afraid. And sometimes people ask a great deal of me as a Christian. And Deborah was asking a great deal of Barak. Asking him to go up against one hundred thousand men and nine hundred iron chariots! After all, he did say he'd go if she'd go with him.

Well, actually, he made it a little stronger than that. What he said was, "If you will go with me, then I will go; *but if you will not go with me, I will not go.*"* And in saying this, he missed a very important point in the conversation.**

Now Deborah was a woman. And she was not a military leader. But with all this against her, she still said, "All right, I'll go with you, *but—*"

"Yes, Deborah? But what?" said Barak.

"But I'm warning you now that the honor of conquering Sisera will go to a woman instead of to you!"

Well, that was that. When you choose not to be a hero, you have to take what comes with it. It's a package deal.

Barak went off to raise his army and prepare for the dreadful day. Horrors, things were as bad as he feared. Only ten thousand men volunteered. What were the chances?

Sisera had a hundred thousand men. How many did the Israelites have? Ten thousand.

Ten to one.

Sisera had nine hundred chariots. How many did the Israelites have? None.

Nine hundred to one.

No, nine hundred to *nothing!*

This was going to be grim business.

When Sisera heard of the Israelites camped on Mount Tabor, he mustered his forces and marched forth to battle. Sisera and his might army! What a sight they made—the nine hundred chariots, the hundred thousand trained warriors, the swords, the shields, the shining armor, the helmets

*Judges 4:8 **(Amplified)**
**Have any idea what it is?

gleaming in the sun—soldiers marching, chariots rumbling, long blades sticking out from their axles—on, on they came, toward the river Kishon.

And the Israelites? What a motley crew *they* were! Farmers and shepherds and tentmakers, fishermen and millers and stonemasons—part-time warriors summoned to battle only in emergency, and certainly no match for Sisera! They had only one advantage. They were camped in hilly country. At least they were UP and Sisera's army was DOWN.

The scene was set for the battle.

Action!!!

"Up!" cried Deborah to Barak, "Arise and get going!"

From the sound of this we might guess that Barak was a little slow in getting started in this attack upon Sisera. And if you are inclined to be hard on Barak, remember that Deborah was doing the *talking* and Barak was doing the *doing*.

"Now is the time for action!" she went on. And Barak roused his men for the march.

"The Lord leads on!"

And Barak started his men down the slopes of Mount Tabor.

"He has already delivered Sisera into your hand!"

And Barak gave the orders to march right into the teeth of the enemy—the trained warriors, the iron chariots, the lethal* knives sticking out from the axle-trees—on, on they came, by the river of Kishon, and then—

RAIN!**

The heavens seemed to open as it poured down! The very earth seemed to tremble and even Mount Carmel seemed to quake as the sheets of rain swept over the land and the River Kishon roared and strained against its banks until its

---

*If you walked into one you were as good as dead.

**Josephus the historian tells us that God threw in a little hail, too.

waters leaped over the sides and lashed against the chariots and the horses of Sisera's army.

Horrors!

The horses whinnied in fear and stood on their hind legs and tangled with each other, and the drivers shouted at them in vain and chariots collided and wheels ground against wheels as they strained and tipped and skidded in the mud.

Panic!

Men ran in confusion, scudding across the battle field, driven before the wind and the blinding rain like leaves with no power of their own.

Pandemonium!*

The chariots ground to a halt, bogged down in the mud, and the charioteers leaped out, tumbling over the foot soldiers, and they all ran for their lives for they were being chased *and Barak's men were doing the chasing!*

Where Is the Fearsome Sisera Now?

The fearsome Sisera leaped from his chariot, deserted his men, and ran for the hills, is what the fearsome Sisera did. He finally stumbled, exhausted, into one of the tents owned by Heber the Kenite. This was friendly territory, he thought, and when Heber's wife Jael invited him in, he was sure of it. He asked her for some water and she gave him a bowl of milk. He lay down to rest and she covered him with a blanket. He fell asleep.

And while he slept, she killed him.

And that's where the fearsome Sisera was now.

He was still there when Barak finally caught up with him.

Barak flung himself into the tent, to kill his enemy. But Deborah had already told him he would not get the credit for killing Sisera—way back there when he'd said he would not go after the Israelites alone.

*A real wing-ding wild uproar.

125

The credit for killing Sisera had gone to a woman. Just as Deborah had said.

This Is the Lord's Doing

The Bible tells us, "So that day the Lord used Israel to subdue King Jabin of Canaan. . . . and Israel became stronger and stronger against King Jabin, until he and all his people were destroyed. After that there was peace in the land for forty years."*

You're Never Alone

There's nothing wrong with the "I'll go if you'll go" business. Sometimes God sends us out in pairs, and even in groups, to get a job done. And often two can do better than one.

The point that Barak missed was that Deborah had said, "*The Lord* has commanded you to do this. And *the Lord* has promised to lead Sisera's army to the Kishon River. And *the Lord* says you will defeat them there."

Ah, ha.

Barak did not want to go alone? Why, *the Lord* was going with him! And he tossed this aside as if it were nothing, and looked at poor little Deborah and said, "I'll go if YOU go with me."

This was his mistake and this was his undoing. He won the victory as God had promised—but the credit went to somebody else.

What About You?

God's promises are the same for you today! So don't quibble and quake and think you're done for without human

*Judges 4:23,24 and 5:31b.

help. If He *does* give you human help, so much the better.

But *don't ever think you're alone without it*. You are not alone. You have God!

And don't forget poor Sisera. He depended on his iron chariots. And where did they wind up?

Stuck in the mud.

13
But I'm a Nobody

Judges 6

"I'm not the sort of person who can 'win friends and influence people.' You couldn't exactly call me a leader. I bungle everything. I'm the sort of person who'd come to class with two-hole paper for a three-hole notebook. In our year book I'd be voted the one 'most likely to be forgotten.' And anyhow, even if I *did* have what it takes to be a leader, there aren't going to be any chances to show it. The whole world's in a mess. And some of the kids' parents say everything is hopeless and there isn't even any sense voting."

Well, that's a pretty glum list of the glooms. The problem is, when you *start* feeling this way, it sort of grows on you, and you keep adding to the list until it grows like Pinocchio's nose—there's no end to it. You'd be way ahead if you'd start your list with the title: "Of course most of these things simply aren't so."

There was a man in the Bible who felt that way. His name was Gideon. He had a gloom-list so long it was a wonder he could even get out of bed in the morning. Trouble was, most of the things on his gloom-list *were* so.

It had been forty years since the Israelites had captured Sisera's army. But now Deborah was gone and Barak was gone and a whole new generation of children had grown up and—

You guessed it. Trouble. They had turned away from God again.

The Bible tells us, "Once again the people of Israel began to worship other gods, and once again the Lord let their enemies harass* them."

This time their chief enemies were the Midianties, and a bad lot *they* were.

They came on camels, hordes of them, more than you could count. And then they robbed and plundered, taking everything they could get their hands on. They stole all the crops the Israelites had planted, they stole their sheep and oxen and donkeys—they did not leave until the land was absolutely stripped. What they did not use up while they were there, they took with them when they left. And cruel? They were so cruel, that the only way to survive was to "head for the hills." This is exactly what many of the Israelites did.

So there they were, living in the hills, hiding their crops from the Midianites, *sneaking around in the very land God had given them.* And there was Gideon in the midst of all this misery, with a gloom-list as long as your arm.

"I'm Not Very Brave"

"When it comes to a show-down, I'm apt to say, 'Let's go —I'm—eh—right behind you.' I'm really not brave at all,

*Their enemies gave them a bad time.

you know—I mean, not at *anything*. Actually I'm afraid of my own shadow."

Well, Gideon was anything but a picture of a brave man. If anyone had called him one, he would have looked behind him to see if the person didn't mean someone else.

When we first hear of him in the Bible, he was not out leading an army against the Midianites; he was on his father's farm, threshing wheat in the winepress. Usually a winepress is used to press grapes, but Gideon was using it to thresh wheat because it was private and out of the way. The Bible tells us he was hiding from the Midianites. So you can see, he did not have a smidgen of derring-do in him at the moment.

It was then that Gideon looked up and saw the stranger. He was sitting under a nearby oak tree. Gideon hadn't seen him come. Suddenly he was just *there*. There was something both eerie and wonderful about it. Was he a prophet perhaps?

Then he spoke.

"The Lord is with you, you mighty man of valor."

Mighty man of valor? All Gideon was doing was whacking at the wheat with a rod.

Gideon looked behind him. There was no one there. The stranger meant *him*.

He shook his head.

"Stranger," he blurted out, "if the Lord is with us, why has all this happened to us? And where are all the miracles our ancestors have told us about—such as when God brought them out of Egypt? Why the Lord has let the Midianites completely ruin us. He has thrown us away!"

He had completely missed the point. But the stranger was patient.

"I will make you strong," he said. "Go and save Israel from the Midianities!"

This was no mere prophet. Was this *the Lord?*

Gideon stared in silence. The stranger looked back at him

131

for a moment. Then—"*I am sending you,*" he said softly.
But it hit Gideon like a thunder-bolt.

"But I'm Not Even Important at Home"

"My brothers and sisters all get more attention than I do.
They're the ones who are full of smarts. They're clever at
outwitting me. And they bring home the best marks and the
highest awards, too. It's like if we were playing *Jacks*—
while I was still on *twosies,* they'd be on *tensies.* We don't
play *Jacks* any more, but you get the idea."

You know, that's just the sort of thing Gideon had in
mind. It was next on his gloom-list. Only he threw in his
whole family for good measure. "Sir," he said, "how can *I*
save Israel? Why the Midianites have robbed us more than
anybody else. My family is the poorest in the whole tribe of
Manasseh. And *I* am the least thought of in the entire family!" Which took care of everybody very nicely. He was
hopeless, his whole family was hopeless, and there was no
use trying because nothing was going to get any better.

Now you just can't get any lower than that. Let the
stranger answer *that* one.

The stranger did.

"But—" he said. What? Was he admitting all these things
were true? Yes, he was admitting all these things were true.
"BUT—"

"But," he said, "You'll destroy the Midianites—and quickly, too. For I, Jehovah, will be with you!"

IT WAS THE LORD!!!

"Can I Believe My Ears?"

"Are all these things I keep hearing about God, really
true? Are the things I hear about Jesus true? I almost feel
like saying, 'Put it in writing.' You know, people say, 'Put it

in writing,' so it'll be *binding,* and you'll know you can depend on it."

Well, for you, he *has* put it in writing. You have the Word of God, the Bible—and it's a personal letter from God to you. *And you can depend on it.*

But in Gideon's day, God was still training His brand-new nation of Israel and Jesus had not come to earth yet and the Holy Spirit had not been sent yet—and without direct *signs,* they just didn't know which way was up. They were like babies, just learning what it was all about!

So Gideon really had a hard time believing his eyes *or* ears!

"If it's really true that you're going to help me like that—then do some miracle to prove it!" he blurted out. "Prove that it is really Jehovah who is talking to me! But wait! Stay here until I go and get an offering for you."

"All right," said the stranger. "I'll stay here until you get back."

Gideon hurried away, his head swimming. If this were true, if this were true— He moved faster than he had in weeks. He came back finally with meat and bread and broth. Could this be the Lord? Could this *really* be the Lord?

"Put the meat and bread on that rock over there," said the stranger, "and pour the broth over it."

Gideon did.

Then the stranger touched the offering with his staff—

FIRE!

It appeared from nowhere, flaming up from the rock!

And the meat crackled and sizzled and the broth hissed, as it all went up in flames. Gideon stared at it in fascination until it was completely consumed, all of it, every smidgen. Then he looked up.

The stranger was gone.

He had not *walked* away. He had absolutely *vanished.*

133

There was absolutely no doubt about it now, no doubt at all.

The Stranger was indeed the Lord!

Gideon was paralyzed with fear.

"It's all right," God told him. "Don't be afraid. You shall not die."

Then, trembling, Gideon started to build an altar to the Lord. His mind went over the strange and wonderful things that had just happened. Over and over and over again, until the altar was finally finished. "Peace with God," he called it.

He felt different than he'd ever felt in his life before.

And he was never, never to be the same again. He'd changed forever, never to turn back.

"But My Parents Aren't Even Christians!"

"It's all right to talk about Gideon, but he wasn't in my situation. My parents aren't Christians and it's hard for me to take a stand. I'll go any place in the world you want me to, but please don't ask me to stand up and be counted at home. I'm a lot better with people who don't know me. Gideon just didn't have this problem."

He didn't?

News for you.

He did.

It was forty years since the glorious days of Deborah and Barak, and the Israelites had turned to idol worship. They had a short memory when it came to God. The minute they didn't have a leader, they ran after false gods at the drop of an idol. So now most of them were worshiping Baal. And guess who was one of the Baal worshipers?

Gideon's *father*. Now the father was the head of the house in those days* and so it's quite probable that the rest of the family were Baal worshipers too. Gideon may have

---

*Womens' Lib hadn't been invented yet.

134

been the only one in the family holding out for God. After all, he *did* say he was the least thought of in his family. If they were Baal worshipers, he must have been doing *something* right.

Did this just knock a crutch from under you?

Well, get up and limp on.

"But I'm Only One Against the Crowd!"

"It isn't just my family, actually. It's the kids at school. And there are even some scoffers in my church crowd. And the kids in my neighborhood. You've no idea how tough it is! I'd rather wait till I build up more confidence."

All of this is true. There's no sense pretending it isn't. And taking a stand is tough. There's no use pretending about that, either.

If God would just stay close to you and keep you comfortable and happy—if He would just let you off the hook—the Christian life would be a picnic.

Yes.

And spineless, too.

And God didn't wait until Gideon had a chance to build up more confidence. God wanted a job done, and He wanted it done "on-the-double." The Bible tells us that *that very night,* the Lord told Gideon to hitch his father's best ox to the family altar of Baal, and pull it down. And to cut down the wooden idol of the goddess Asherah that stood nearby. And to build a new altar—to the Lord! And to offer a sacrifice on it. *To the Lord.* What to use for the sacrifice? Why the ox of course. What to use for the fire to burn the ox? Why the wooden idol, of course. Which did a pretty thorough job of putting idol-worship in its place!

It was a hard thing to do. But Gideon did it. He took ten of his servants, and they sneaked out in the night and got the whole job done while it was dark. Gideon had met the

Lord, he had obeyed the Lord, and now he was "on his way."

Now if Gideon had any idea that the Lord had promised him a bed of roses, he was soon to realize that this just wasn't so. That the Lord would be with Him? Yes. That he would have a bed of roses? Not necessarily. For early the next morning, all the Baal worshipers in the village were clamoring at his father's door.

"Send out your son!" they yelled, "Send out Gideon! For he has insulted the altar of Baal! He has cut down the Asherah idol!"

Did they want to talk to Gideon?

No. They wanted to *kill* him. They weren't fooling around.

Then something very interesting happened. Someone came to Gideon's rescue.

Gideon's *father*.

Gideon's father not only rescued him, but he was pretty shrewd about it. "Does Baal need *your* help?" he yelled back, "What an insult to a god!" And the crowd got quiet. "If Baal is really a god, let him take care of himself! Let *him* destroy whoever broke his altar down!"

Pretty clever answer, what?

Indeed it was. It was clever enough to stop them. And off they went, without doing him any harm. From then on Gideon had a nickname. It was "Jerubbaal," and it meant "Let Baal take care of himself!"

What? His job was done already? Not on your life. The hardest part was yet to come.

The pesky Midianites were swooping down, on another expedition of piracy!

"But I Still Have All These Doubts"

"I really wanted to go all out for You, Lord, and I started out thinking You were leading me—but now I'm not so

136

sure. I'm not sure about anything. Sometimes the things I thought You wanted me to do on Sunday, I'm not so sure of by Thursday. The doubts creep in and I get to feeling queasy about it. What's wrong with me? Am I just wishy-washy?"

Not at all. Gideon had his doubts too. He started off with flying colors.

"Call to arms!"

Yes, it was Gideon, blowing a trumpet and calling the Israelites to fight back!

He called the men of his own clan* first, and they got organized. They sent messengers to the rest of their tribe**— and then to several other tribes, calling for their fighting forces. And they all responded! On and on they came, thousands of them, ready to fight! And Gideon was the leader!

Good grief.

That is when the doubts began to creep in. Gideon began to drag his feet.

Gideon wasn't ashamed of them, though. He came right out with them, in fact. And he asked God to just spell it out! Was it or wasn't it? Should he or shouldn't he? What was the score?

"Lord," he said, "If You are really going to use me to save Israel, prove it! I'll put some wool on the threshing floor tonight. And when the morning comes, if the fleece is wet *but the ground is dry*—then I'll know for sure that You are going to help me."

Gideon probably slept very little that night. Would God really do what he asked?

In the morning he got stuck in doorways, getting to that wool. The ground was dry all right—but the wool, the wool! Would it be wet?

He picked it up with trembling hands.

*Group of families.
**Which was the tribe of Manasseh, remember?

It was *dripping!* It was so wet, he wrung out a whole bowlful of water!

Now you'd think this would be enough proof, but it wasn't. You've heard of people who are fond of saying, "You've got to show me." Well, Gideon was one of those chaps who said, "You've got to show me—and show me—*and show me.*"

He was *still* dragging his feet.

"Lord," he said, "please don't be angry with me*—let me make one more test. I'll leave some wool out again. And this time, let the wool stay dry—while the ground all around it is wet!"

Preposterous!**

But, preposterous or not, Gideon asked it. And he put the wool out—and waited. And the next morning—

The wool was as dry as an old bone in the sun. But the ground all around was wet with dew!

Well, that did it. There could be no mistake. God was with him. He could not fail.

Every doubt Gideon had, God had knocked down. And every question Gideon had, God had answered. How could he hang back now, when God had so clearly said, "Go do it." There was no way to go but forward. And forward. Gideon decided to go. And that's how it happened that Gideon did the unthinkable.

Was he equal to the task?

No. But God *was.*

What About You?

Do you still feel like a nobody?

It could be that you are fortunate. For those are the kinds of persons God likes to use. "I will be with you," He says.

*He had the sense to know he was being a bit of a bore.
**This was really going overboard!

138

And that makes you *somebody!*

"For when I am weak (by myself) then am I strong (in Christ)."*

*2 Corinthians 12:10

14
Ouch! My Doubts!

Judges 7 and 8

"I'd Rather Do It Myself"

Well, it's great to accomplish things on your own. You *want* to "do it yourself." That's the way you were trained from babyhood. From the moment you took your first spill —after you'd graduated from babyhood and got to be a "little kid"—your parents, instead of running to pick you up, told you to do it yourself. And after a while, you got the idea. It was just the thing to do.

"But," you say, "Doesn't God want me to be independent, stand on my own?" Of course He does. He wants you to grow up, stand up, measure up, and all the rest of it. And that's the point. You can't do it, according to His standards,* by yourself.

Gideon knew now what the Lord wanted him to do.** He had talked with the Lord and "put out the fleece." Now there was no longer any doubt about it. God wanted him to lead the Israelites against their enemies.

*More about that later.
**What? You don't know about this? Go back and read chapter thirteen!

What an army he had! They came pouring in from all parts of the country. They seemed to be coming out of the very cracks of the earth. They came out of caves and streamed down the mountain passes, and sneaked across the plains. Five thousand, ten thousand, fifteen thousand—could this be possible? Yes! Twenty thousand, twenty-five thousand, thirty thousand—and, when all heads were counted—thirty-two thousand men! "This is almost too good to be true," thought Gideon. "With thirty-two thousand men, we'll wipe the Midianites off the face of the earth!"

As soon as they could get organized, he got his army off to an early start, and they marched as far as the spring of Harod. The Midianites and their allies* were camped just to the north of them, down in the valley. "We'll *pulverize* them," thought Gideon.

And then God said something that made Gideon stop in his tracks.

"Gideon," the Lord said, "there are too many of you. Your army is too big."

What?!?

Could the Lord really mean this? Why with an army like this, they couldn't fail.

That was just the point.

The trouble with the army was, that it was too big.

"I can't let all of you fight the Midianites," the Lord said, "for then the people of Israel will boast to me that they saved themselves by their own strength!"

Well then, what to do?

"Issue orders that anyone who is timid about this venture, may go home."

Well this was a bit of a jolt. The Midianites were fierce

*Guys on their side.

and cruel. And Gideon didn't want to lose a man—*not one*. He needed every man he could get. Suppose five hundred of them went home? What a loss! Suppose a thousand left— five thousand—it would be a disaster!

Horrors!

Then the men started to leave. And they kept leaving— and leaving—and leaving—and leaving—

Good grief. It didn't seem possible. It couldn't be so.

But it was so. It seemed like a nightmare, and before it was over, twenty-two thousand of them had left! And in anybody's arithmetic, twenty-two thousand from thirty-two thousand leaves—oh, no!

Only ten thousand men left?

Yes. Only ten thousand men left.

"What Are You Up To?"

"Lord, I not only wanted You to help me, but I was willing and eager for You to help me. But I had my plans all made and I did sort of want to do it myself in my own way. I do appreciate Your help, but You *do* seem to be twisting my plans up a bit."

Well, God seemed to be twisting Gideon's plans up a bit too. He'd started out with an army of thirty-two thousand men, and now this! What *was* God up to? Leaving only a measly ten thousand men! Why they weren't enough to—

And then the Lord told Gideon something that shocked him right out of his sandals.

"There are still too many," He said.

"Lord, Are You Absolutely Sure You Know What You're Doing?"

Of course we may not come right out and say this. We might not even admit that we even *thought* it. But if we're honest we have to admit that there are times when the

143

thought does cross our minds that the Lord just might be a bit fuzzy about what He's doing.

The next thing the Lord said must have left Gideon's mouth sagging open. After all, for forty years the Israelites had been out of touch with God, so this was a brand new experience. As far as faith was concerned, they *were* a little bit out of practice.

"Bring them down to the spring and have them drink," the Lord told Gideon. "And all the men who cup the water in their hands to get it to their mouths, will go with you. And all the men who kneel and drink with their mouths in the stream—away they go. Send them home."

Well, Gideon gave the orders. And ten thousand men went down to the water. Some of them laid down all their weapons and got right down on their knees and put their mouths in the water and drank like there was no tomorrow. Any enemy could have sneaked up on them and—POW!

They would never have known what hit them.

But there were some who didn't stop to do that. They just stooped and took water in their cupped hands, their eyes on swivels, looking in all directions. No enemy could have surprised them. They were ready for anything.

And the Lord said, "The ones who are drinking as they stand—watchful and ready to fight—are the ones to go with you."

The ones with their eyes on swivels numbered only three hundred!

"I'll conquer the Midianites with these three hundred!" the Lord said. "Send the others home."

Only three hundred left!

Good grief.

Remember?

Then suddenly all the pieces began to fall into place. And everything began to make sense.

Of course!

God was the God of the impossible. And this was the way He did things. Why the whole history of the Israelites proved that this was the way He did things. He had made a path through the Red Sea, He had given them water out of a rock, He had made a path through the Jordan, He had sent the walls of Jericho crashing down the hillsides. He had stretched one day almost as long as two, He had caused the wheels of Barak's chariots to get besoggled in the mud—

Yes, indeed. He was the God of the impossible. And this was beginning to look like old times.

How wonderful.

"Ouch! My Doubts!"

"But even after I've seen some of the wonderful things God can do, I find myself doubting. Just when I think I'm all set, the doubts come pussy-footing back, sneaking into my mind. Not big doubts, usually. Just pesky little ones. What's wrong with me?"

There's nothing wrong with you, so don't feel guilty about it. Doubting is a very part of your nature—it's the way you're made. God understands this in you. Be honest with Him. Tell Him about those pesky doubts.

That's what Gideon must have done.

"What? Gideon still afraid? Did *he* have doubts again?"

He must have been afraid. And it's pretty easy to understand why. In spite of all the marvelous things that had happened to him, he was still a farmer, not a warrior. He was no great general, and he knew it. And here he was, up in the hills in the dark with three hundred men, and about to go to war against the Midianites. And there were so many of *them* they couldn't be counted! It was enough to make any poor Israelite shiver in his sandals. Now God understood fear in Gideon just as He understands fear in you. "Get up," He told Gideon, "and take your troops—"

145

(*Troops?* Only three hundred men? Auuuuuuugh!) "—take your troops, and attack the Midianites. I'm going to cause you to defeat them. *But—*"

And here's where God showed Himself to be a loving Father. He was about to give Gideon a little encouragement, a pat on the back. Everybody needs that once in awhile. The non-heroes, and the heroes like Gideon. "But—if you are afraid, just go down to the enemy camp alone. Or you may take along your servant Purah if you want to. But go down there and listen to what they are saying. I think you'll feel a lot better. In fact, I think you'll be eager to get going."

Well, *that* was a twist.

Gideon got a hold of his servant Purah, and the two of them crept down through the darkness to the outposts of the enemy camp. The Midianite army was scattered all over the valley, as far as eye could see. In the dark they looked spooky, shadows on the sand. And the camels, sulky and bad-smelling,* were crouched in the dark, big bumps in the sand, and there were so many of them they looked like miles and miles of bumps.

Gideon and Purah crept along in the darkness and—

Wait a minute. What was this?

There were voices inside one of the tents.

Gideon crept closer. And listened.

Down Goes the Last Doubt!

Oh, oh. One of the men had had a nightmare, and he was telling his tent-mate about it "I had the strangest dream," he said. "It seemed like there was this huge loaf of barley bread. And it came tumbling down from somewhere, toward our camp. And it hit our tent—this one—and knocked it flat!" There was silence. They seemed to be thinking

*Camels always look as if they'd just had a snort of vinegar, and they smell **terrible**.

about this for a minute. Then suddenly it hit them. A barley loaf! Why barley was a second-rate grain—it was only half the price of wheat. Barley loaf. Why that was the nickname for a farmer boy—a country bumpkin!

GIDEON!!!

And they cried, "That can mean only one thing. Gideon the Israelite—he's going to come down here and wipe us out! The God of Israel has delivered us into Gideon's hands!"

It was unbelievable!

Gideon could only stand there and worship God in the dark.

Then, with Purah, he scrambled back up the hill. His little army of three hundred suddenly looked great to him. His last doubt vanished in the darkness.

Get Up and Get Going!

"Get up!" Gideon told his army. "Get up and get going! For the Lord is going to use you to conquer the enemy tonight!"

They woke each other up, and the word was passed throughout Gideon's little camp. That little band of three hundred was going to conquer that frightening mass of men and camels down in the valley!

"Here are the battle plans," said Gideon. He divided the three hundred men into three groups—a hundred men in each group. Then their "ammunition" was passed out to them. And the "ammunition" was something you wouldn't believe. They probably had a hard time believing it too. Each man got a ram's-horn trumpet. And a clay pitcher with a torch in it.*

That was all?

*The practice of concealing a lamp or a torch in a pitcher is still known in Egypt.

147

That was all.

"Just do as I do, when we get there," Gideon told them. Then he proceeded to outline the battle plan and told them exactly what he was going to do. Then they started down the hill for one of the strangest battles that ever took place.

See the Lord Work!

The three hundred men sneaked down in the darkness. Quietly, quietly. They broke up into three groups, a hundred men in each. They sneaked around the edges of the camp. It was just after midnight. It was the beginning of a new watch, and the sentries coming on duty were still puffy-eyed from sleep. Their eyes weren't too good in the dark yet. Quiet, quiet—not a sound—they stopped if even a twig snapped.

Finally they were ready.

Gideon gave the signal. And every man sprang into action!

CRASH!

They smashed their clay pitchers!

FLASH!

They held their torches high. And the darkness was suddenly blazing with three hundred torches!

BLAST!

They blew their trumpets loud and clear. And they shouted, "For the Lord and Gideon!!!" with a shout that split the skies!

The Midianite soldiers scrambled out of their tents. Lights! Lights! Everywhere they looked! And noise! The blare of the trumpets and the shouting bounced against the surrounding hills—and the noise and the lights seemed to fill the whole earth! The combination blasted their ears and blinded their eyes and curdled their blood.

The enemy seemed to be on all sides. How many were there? Thousands? Hundreds of thousands?*

The commanding officers screamed, "At 'em!"

At *who!*

At *anybody!*

And then—

PANDEMONIUM!**

There was no order. Just confusion and fright. They fought with each other, they killed each other from one end of the camp to the other. They ran around in circles. And then they ran blindly off into the night.

Gideon sent messengers to all the surrounding Israelite tribes, to head them off—so no matter which direction they fled, they were caught. Not one of them escaped.

It was a smashing, crashing, dashing victory.

But it was the Lord's victory. No doubt about it.

And that's how it happened that poor trembling Gideon (who thought he was a nobody) became a hero.

You're No Hero?

Well let's see what the dictionary has to say about the word "hero."

> Hero: A hero is a man (or a woman!) of courage and ability admired for his brave deeds and noble qualities, and is regarded as a model, or ideal.

It does *not* say that a hero never loses his temper, is never afraid, never get spells of being wish-washy, never wonders if God is really with him, never has any doubts—and never asks any questions.

You always thought a hero was somebody who was just about perfect? And never had any fears? Or faults?

---

*It sounded like impossibadrillions!

**Not just ordinary panic. Super-panic. A real wild uproar. Good word. Try it on your parents.

What Nonsense!

Take the heroes in this book. Every doubt that you have had, they had. Every question that you have had, they had. And if you had really known them personally you might find that every hang-up you have had, they had. They didn't have all of them all of the time, but they sure did have some of them some of the time!

What made them heroes is that they had these weaknesses, and somehow went ahead and got the job done anyway. They just plunged in with all their doubts and all their questions and all their weaknesses—and trusted God.

You might feel like a nobody, but He has promised, "I will be with you." And that makes you *somebody*.

Here's a verse to live by: "Commit thy way unto the Lord, trust also in Him, and HE will bring it to pass."* This is what God was trying to teach the heroes in this book. This is what He is trying to teach you.

"Who, Me?"

Yes, you there, ready to put this book down.** There's still a great deal of work to be done. And God is still looking for people to do it. "For the eyes of the Lord search back and forth across the whole earth, looking for people whose hearts are perfect toward him, so that he can show his great power in helping them."***

There, you have it—in writing!

God is looking for YOU!

*Psalm 37:5
**And I hope you've read it all!
***2 Chronicles 16:9, TLB

19-100